Engaging Learners at All Levels
How Adapting Elementary Strategies Can Transform Secondary Education

Dr. Pamela T. Chandler

© 2025 Dr. Pamela T. Chandler
All rights reserved.
No part of this book may be reproduced without written permission from the publisher, except for brief quotations used in reviews or in academic work.

Published by Instructional Impact, LLC
ISBN: 979-8-9940764-0-8
Printed in the United States of America
First Edition

This book reflects professional experience and personal insights. It is not intended to replace district policy or state guidelines. All examples of students, teachers, and schools are either shared with consent or presented in a general way.

For every educator who believes students can grow with the right support, and for every student who deserves learning that meets their needs.

INTRODUCTION: WHY SECONDARY SCHOOLS NEED TO RECONNECT WITH ELEMENTARY STRATEGIES 1

CHAPTER 1: THE POWER OF ENGAGEMENT – CONNECTING WITH EVERY STUDENT 3

CHAPTER 2: VISUAL LEARNING – WHY SECONDARY CLASSROOMS SHOULD BE VIBRANT 11

CHAPTER 3: PERSONALIZATION – MAKING LEARNING RELEVANT FOR EVERY STUDENT 18

CHAPTER 4: FROM LECTURE TO INTERACTION – CREATING ACTIVE LEARNING SPACES 25

CHAPTER 5: CLASSROOM MANAGEMENT IN THE HIGH SCHOOL CLASSROOM – STRUCTURING SUCCESS THROUGH ENGAGEMENT AND CONSISTENCY 32

CHAPTER 6: MANIPULATIVES, ANCHOR CHARTS, AND OTHER TOOLS FOR UNDERSTANDING AT ANY AGE 37

CHAPTER 7: VOCABULARY WALLS AND WORD WALLS – BUILDING LANGUAGE AT EVERY LEVEL 44

CHAPTER 8: THE POWER OF GROUPED SEATING – COLLABORATIVE LEARNING IN SECONDARY CLASSROOMS 51

CHAPTER 9: READ-ALOUDS – ENGAGING MINDS ACROSS ALL AGES 58

CHAPTER 10: HIGHLIGHTERS, POST-ITS, AND INTERACTIVE NOTEBOOKS – CREATING TOOLS FOR ACTIVE LEARNING 65

CHAPTER 11: USING DATA TO INFORM INSTRUCTION 72

CHAPTER 12: CHECKING FOR UNDERSTANDING – STRATEGIES TO GAUGE STUDENT LEARNING 79

CHAPTER 13: SMALL GROUP INSTRUCTION – TAILORING LEARNING TO MEET STUDENT NEEDS 86

CHAPTER 14: BUILDING STRONGER CONNECTIONS – EFFECTIVE COMMUNICATION WITH STUDENTS AND PARENTS 99

CHAPTER 15: MODELING AND THINKING ALOUD – MAKING THE INVISIBLE THINKING PROCESS VISIBLE 107

CHAPTER 16: IMPLEMENTING CHANGE – OVERCOMING RESISTANCE TO ADAPTING ELEMENTARY STRATEGIES IN SECONDARY EDUCATION 114

CONCLUSION: BRINGING IT ALL TOGETHER – THE POWER OF RECONNECTING ELEMENTARY STRATEGIES TO SECONDARY EDUCATION 121

ACKNOWLEDGMENTS 135

ABOUT THE AUTHOR 136

Preface

Teachers often enter the secondary classroom with strong content knowledge, yet many feel that student engagement and connection are harder to build. My work across grade levels has shown that strategies used in elementary classrooms can support learning at every age. These strategies help students stay active in the lesson, understand the purpose of each task, and take ownership of their progress.

This book offers ideas that you can use right away. You will see clear examples from real classrooms and practical steps that support instruction. The goal is simple. Help you create lessons and learning spaces where students stay active, participate with purpose, and understand what they are learning.

Engaging Learners at all Levels: How Adapting Elementary Strategies Can Transform and Elevate Secondary Education by Dr. Pamela Chandler

Introduction: Why Secondary Schools Need to Reconnect with Elementary Strategies

For many educators, the transition from elementary to secondary education feels like a move into a more serious, structured environment where the stakes are higher and the students are older. As a result, many teachers in middle and high school classrooms believe that strategies designed for younger students, such as bright visuals, interactive activities, and personalized learning, are no longer necessary. However, this assumption couldn't be further from the truth.

In reality, when we examine secondary classrooms, we see a noticeable gap. Too often, the rich engagement techniques that are second nature in elementary schools, such as decorated classrooms, vocabulary walls, hands-on manipulatives, and student-centered activities, are missing in middle and high school settings. Instead, these classrooms often rely heavily on lecture-based teaching, where students passively receive information rather than actively engaging with it. This approach is problematic because we know that when students are actively involved in their learning, they retain more, are more motivated, and are more likely to succeed academically.

As educators, we must recognize that the needs of secondary students aren't much different from those of younger learners. Adolescents still need to be engaged, challenged, and supported in ways that speak to their individual learning styles and interests. They may be older, but they still benefit from the same strategies that make elementary classrooms so effective: personalization, active learning, collaborative work, and meaningful engagement.

"Engaging Learners at all Levels: How Adapting Elementary Strategies Can Transform and Elevate Secondary Education" aims to explore how we can take the proven strategies used in elementary education and adapt them for secondary classrooms. It's about recognizing that these strategies aren't just for young students. They work for all students. By bringing these methods into middle and high school classrooms, we can create a learning environment that is dynamic, engaging, and supportive of every student.

In this book, you will discover how to shift your classroom from a passive learning space to an active, student-centered environment. You will see how strategies like visuals, manipulatives, collaborative seating, and interactive activities can be adapted for secondary students. You will also learn how techniques such as read-alouds, anchor charts, and highlighter strategies can elevate content instruction in middle and high school settings. Most importantly, you will understand how these approaches, rooted in the heart of elementary education, can have a profound instructional impact on students of all ages.

The following chapters will provide practical insights and examples of how these strategies can be seamlessly integrated into your classroom, no matter the grade level you teach. Whether you are an experienced educator or just starting your teaching journey, this book will offer you the tools to create a more engaging, inclusive, and effective learning environment.

Secondary education doesn't have to be disconnected from the heart of teaching. It's time to embrace the strategies that work for all students and elevate our classrooms to meet the diverse needs of our learners. By adapting elementary techniques, we can cultivate a classroom environment that encourages engagement, critical thinking, and student growth, no matter the grade level.

Chapter 1: The Power of Engagement – Connecting with Every Student

In every classroom, engagement is the key to success. It's the spark that ignites students' interest and motivates them to take an active role in their learning. Yet, in many middle and high school classrooms, student engagement is often treated as an afterthought, overshadowed by the emphasis on content delivery and testing. This is a critical oversight, as engagement is the driving force behind not only academic achievement but also emotional investment in learning.

In elementary classrooms, engagement is central to the learning process. Teachers use a variety of methods to capture students' attention and make learning enjoyable. Bright visuals, hands-on activities, flexible seating arrangements, and personalized learning experiences are just some of the ways elementary teachers engage their students. Unfortunately, as students advance to middle and high school, many of these strategies are abandoned in favor of lecture-based instruction, where students are expected to absorb information passively. This shift often leads to disengagement, and over time, students may become less motivated and less willing to participate.

What if we reimagine the secondary classroom as one that values engagement just as much as elementary classrooms do? What if we believe that older students, like their younger counterparts, deserve learning experiences that actively involve them, that are dynamic and interactive?

The truth is that secondary students need engagement just as much as younger students do. In fact, research shows that when students are actively engaged in their learning, they retain information better, develop deeper understanding, and feel more connected to the content and the teacher. Engagement leads to intrinsic motivation, which fuels a desire to learn for the sake of learning, rather than simply to perform well on tests.

Engagement in middle and high school looks different than it does in elementary classrooms, but the principles remain the same. When we engage students in their learning, we create an environment that fosters collaboration, critical thinking, and creativity. We give students the opportunity to take ownership of their education, to make connections between what they are learning and the world around them. We offer them the space to explore new ideas, ask questions, and develop the skills they need to succeed, not only in school but in life.

To engage secondary students, we need to bring back the practices that work: active learning strategies, personalization, collaboration, and hands-on experiences. These are the same techniques that teachers use in elementary classrooms to make learning feel relevant and exciting. The beauty of these strategies is that they are adaptable and can be tailored to meet the needs of middle and high school students.

In this chapter, we will explore how to make engagement a cornerstone of your secondary classroom. We'll look at how to create an atmosphere where students feel excited to learn, where they are actively involved in the process, and where their contributions are valued. You'll learn how to use interactive lessons, group work, and real-world applications to help students connect with the material in a meaningful way. We'll also discuss how to personalize learning to cater to different learning styles and interests, ensuring that every student feels included and challenged.

Most importantly, we'll explore how the power of engagement can transform your classroom. When students are engaged, they are motivated to do their best, and their success becomes not just a goal for them, but a shared achievement for the entire classroom community.

Engagement is not just a teaching strategy; it is the foundation for building relationships with students, nurturing their academic growth, and helping them develop a lifelong love of learning. By embracing the power of engagement, we can create classrooms that are vibrant, student-centered spaces where all students can thrive.

Creating an Exciting and Inviting Classroom Environment

The first step in fostering engagement is creating an atmosphere where students feel welcomed, safe, and eager to participate. This begins with the physical space of the classroom. In elementary schools, classrooms are often vibrant, with decorations, visual aids, and student work adorning the walls. These elements not only make the space more visually appealing but also help students feel connected to their learning environment. For secondary classrooms, we can adapt this concept by creating an inviting, interactive space that sparks curiosity.

- **Classroom layout and seating arrangements:** Rather than traditional rows of desks facing the front, try organizing your classroom in a way that promotes interaction. Group seating arrangements or flexible seating options allow students to work together and engage in collaborative learning experiences. This seating structure encourages communication and fosters a sense of community, where students feel they have a voice and can contribute to group discussions.
- **Decor and student work:** Your classroom can be visually stimulating without being overwhelming. Consider displaying student work, anchor charts, and content-related visuals. These visuals not only make the space more inviting

but also serve as useful references that students can turn to for support. Over time, these displays will evolve, creating a sense of ownership as students contribute to the learning environment.

Active Learning Strategies and Interactive Lessons

Engagement thrives when students are actively involved in their learning, rather than passively receiving information. One of the most effective ways to increase student engagement is through active learning strategies. These strategies shift the focus from the teacher to the students, encouraging them to participate in meaningful ways.

- **Interactive lessons:** Interactive lessons involve students in the process of learning through discussion, hands-on activities, or problem-solving tasks. These lessons move beyond traditional lectures, offering opportunities for students to explore concepts on their own and in groups. Consider incorporating activities like debates, case studies, or project-based learning. By using these strategies, you give students a chance to interact with the content and with each other in a way that promotes critical thinking and deeper understanding.
- **Group work:** Group work is an essential tool for building engagement in secondary classrooms. It provides students with the chance to collaborate, problem-solve, and learn from one another. In groups, students can share ideas, challenge each other's thinking, and work together to reach a common goal. By giving students autonomy in their groups, you allow them to take ownership of their learning and engage in peer-to-peer teaching. Group work also helps build communication and social skills that are critical in the modern world.

- **Real-world applications:** Students often struggle to connect what they are learning in the classroom to the real world. One way to combat this is by integrating real-world applications into your lessons. When students see how the concepts they are studying are relevant to their lives, they become more motivated to engage with the material. For example, in a math class, you might ask students to work on budgeting a personal project, or in a science class, you could explore current environmental issues. By bringing in real-world contexts, you help students see the value in what they are learning and how it applies beyond the classroom.

Personalizing Learning to Cater to Diverse Needs

Not all students learn in the same way, and engagement is most effective when learning is personalized to cater to the diverse needs of students. Personalization allows you to meet students where they are and provide them with the tools and opportunities they need to succeed.

- **Differentiation:** Differentiating instruction is key to personalizing learning. This means tailoring your teaching methods, materials, and assessments to the varying needs, interests, and abilities of your students. For example, some students might need extra support through visual aids, while others might benefit from more hands-on, kinesthetic learning experiences. By differentiating your approach, you ensure that every student has access to the material in a way that is meaningful to them.
- **Learning styles and interests:** Pay attention to the individual learning styles of your students. Some may be auditory learners, others may prefer visual or tactile experiences. By providing a variety of materials and activities, such as videos, hands-on projects, or group

discussions, you allow students to engage with the content in a way that suits their strengths. Additionally, by incorporating students' personal interests into lessons, you create a more relevant and motivating learning experience. If a student loves music, for example, you could introduce math problems related to rhythm or sound.

The Transformative Power of Engagement

Engagement does more than make the classroom a more enjoyable place to learn. It has the power to transform your teaching and your students' learning experiences. When students are engaged, they become active participants in their education. They begin to see themselves as capable learners who are responsible for their own success. This shift in mindset leads to greater motivation, increased academic achievement, and a sense of community within the classroom.

- **Motivation and achievement:** Engagement and motivation are intrinsically linked. When students are actively involved in the learning process, they are more likely to put forth the effort necessary to succeed. Engagement fosters a sense of purpose and ownership, making students more invested in their learning. This intrinsic motivation leads to higher levels of academic achievement, as students are more willing to take risks, ask questions, and persist in the face of challenges.
- **A shared achievement:** When a classroom is truly engaged, success is not just the result of individual effort but of collective collaboration. As students work together, they celebrate each other's accomplishments and share in the pride of their collective success. This creates a classroom culture where students feel supported and encouraged, and where learning becomes a shared journey.

In conclusion, the power of engagement is transformative. By creating an environment where students are excited to learn, actively involved in the process, and given opportunities to personalize their learning, you can foster a classroom where every student thrives. Engagement isn't just about making learning fun, it's about empowering students to take ownership of their education and helping them realize their full potential. Through interactive lessons, group work, real-world applications, and personalized learning, you can create a classroom where students are motivated to do their best, and where their success becomes a shared achievement for the entire community.

You try it!: Create opportunities for student interaction by incorporating collaborative activities like group presentations, hands-on experiments, or peer-to-peer teaching. These activities can help students feel more invested in their learning by giving them agency and involving them in the process. Try organizing group discussions or debates on relevant topics to get students actively involved in the material.

Chapter 2: Visual Learning – Why Secondary Classrooms Should Be Vibrant

When we think of a classroom that engages students, we often imagine a space filled with bright posters, interactive displays, and student work that covers the walls. For many, this image is associated with elementary classrooms, where visual learning tools are an essential part of the daily routine. But why should these visual strategies be limited to younger students? Secondary students can benefit from the same vibrant learning environment that uses visuals to support, clarify, and enhance their understanding.

Visuals are more than just decorations, they are tools that can deepen student learning. Research consistently shows that students retain information better when they can see it, especially when the visuals are paired with verbal or written explanations. Secondary students, despite being older, still process information in ways that can be made clearer and more meaningful with the help of visuals. In this chapter, we will explore why visual learning is crucial for secondary classrooms and how you can incorporate visuals to support students in their journey of understanding.

The Power of Visual Learning

At its core, visual learning is about presenting information in ways that support students' ability to absorb and process new ideas. When secondary students are presented with complex concepts, whether in math, science, history, or literature, they often struggle to make connections between the abstract and the concrete. Visual aids can help bridge this gap, making the information more accessible, understandable, and memorable.

- **Cognitive benefits of visuals:** Visual learning helps engage the brain's visual processing centers, reinforcing what students are hearing and reading. By presenting content in a

visual format, you provide students with an alternative way to process information, which can be particularly beneficial for those who are visual learners. This multimodal approach, combining visual, auditory, and kinesthetic input, has been shown to increase retention and understanding.
- **Supporting diverse learning styles:** In any classroom, there are a variety of learning styles. Some students may struggle with traditional lecture-based instruction and find it hard to process information through listening alone. By incorporating visuals, such as charts, diagrams, videos, and infographics, you offer students multiple entry points into the content. This makes it easier for all students, regardless of learning style, to engage with and retain the material.

Why Secondary Classrooms Should Be Visual

In secondary education, where the content becomes more abstract and specialized, the need for visual learning tools becomes even more important. At this stage, students are expected to grasp more complex ideas, but without the support of visuals, these concepts can seem distant or overwhelming.

- **Making abstract concepts concrete:** Whether teaching algebra, physics, or literary analysis, secondary educators are often faced with the challenge of making abstract ideas more tangible. Visuals can make these concepts more concrete and relatable. A well-placed diagram in a science classroom can illustrate a complex process, such as the water cycle, and give students a clearer understanding of the topic. In history, a timeline can help students visualize events in a chronological order, making it easier to grasp the relationships between events and their significance.
- **Visuals as memory aids:** For secondary students, the sheer volume of content they need to learn can feel overwhelming.

One way to help them retain more information is by using visual cues that serve as memory aids. A vocabulary wall with key terms, or an anchor chart summarizing key concepts, can help students recall important information during class discussions or tests. These visuals act as reference points, reinforcing the content and helping students organize their thoughts.

Practical Ways to Integrate Visuals into Secondary Classrooms

Incorporating visuals into your classroom doesn't require a complete overhaul of your teaching methods, but rather a thoughtful integration of different types of visual aids that enhance learning. Here are some practical ways you can use visuals in your secondary classroom:

- **Anchor charts:** Anchor charts are a staple in elementary classrooms, but they can be just as effective in secondary classrooms. Use anchor charts to display important concepts, processes, or strategies that students can refer to throughout the unit. For example, a math teacher might use an anchor chart to show step-by-step problem-solving strategies, while a history teacher might create a chart outlining the causes and effects of a historical event. These charts serve as living resources that students can reference and add to as they deepen their understanding.
- **Infographics and diagrams:** Infographics are a great way to present information visually in a concise and engaging way. Use infographics to explain complex topics or to present data in a more digestible format. Diagrams, whether in science or social studies, can help students visualize processes, structures, or relationships between concepts. Consider using a flowchart to explain a sequence of events or a Venn diagram to compare and contrast two ideas.

- **Visual note-taking:** Encourage students to incorporate visuals into their own note-taking. Visual note-taking, sometimes referred to as sketchnoting, can help students synthesize and organize their thoughts. Encourage students to draw diagrams, charts, or symbols that represent key ideas in the lesson. This allows them to connect words with images, making the content more meaningful and memorable.
- **Interactive visuals:** To make visuals even more engaging, consider incorporating interactive elements. This might include digital tools that allow students to manipulate visuals, such as online diagrams or virtual whiteboards where students can collaborate. Interactive visuals also extend to group activities where students create their own visuals as part of a project. This hands-on approach reinforces the concepts and encourages student ownership of their learning.

Beyond the Classroom – Visual Learning in the Real World

The power of visual learning extends beyond the classroom. In the real world, visuals play a significant role in how we communicate and process information. Think about the last time you looked at a map, a news graphic, or an infographic on social media. These visuals helped you understand complex information quickly and effectively. By integrating visual learning into secondary classrooms, we are preparing students to navigate a world where visual literacy is increasingly important.

- **Visual literacy:** Visual literacy is the ability to interpret, create, and understand visual messages. In today's society, students must be able to interpret charts, graphs, and visual data in a variety of contexts, from news reports to business presentations. By teaching students to analyze and create visuals, we are equipping them with a skill set that will serve them beyond the classroom.

- **Real-world application of visual learning:** In the workplace, visuals are used to communicate ideas, share data, and make complex concepts accessible to a broad audience. By incorporating visual learning strategies in the classroom, we help students develop the skills they need to succeed in careers that demand strong visual communication abilities, such as marketing, design, data analysis, and more.

Creating a Vibrant Learning Environment

The classroom environment plays a crucial role in fostering engagement. By making secondary classrooms visually rich and interactive, we create a space where students are more likely to feel inspired and motivated to learn. This environment not only supports students' understanding but also reflects the value placed on their learning experience.

- **Encouraging creativity and expression:** When students see that their classroom is a place where learning is dynamic and creative, they are more likely to feel excited about the material. Consider providing opportunities for students to create their own visual representations of what they are learning. This could include designing posters, creating infographics, or drawing diagrams that represent key concepts. These activities not only engage students but also give them a sense of ownership over their learning.
- **Classroom displays:** Displaying students' work in the classroom helps them feel valued and reinforces the idea that they are active participants in the learning process. Create a space where students can showcase their visual projects, whether it's a poster, a chart, or a piece of artwork related to the lesson. This promotes a sense of pride and achievement, and it encourages students to take an active role in contributing to the classroom community.

Visuals are not just for younger students, they are a powerful tool for learning at any age. By embracing the use of visuals in your secondary classroom, you can support diverse learning styles, clarify complex concepts, and foster a more engaging and dynamic learning environment. As you integrate visual learning into your lessons, you will see firsthand how these tools can enhance student understanding, increase retention, and create a vibrant, student-centered classroom.

You try it! Incorporate visual tools like timelines, mind maps, and concept charts in your lessons. When covering a new topic, display visuals on the board or create handouts that highlight key ideas in color-coded sections. Encourage students to create their own visuals during note-taking to help reinforce their understanding.

Chapter 3: Personalization – Making Learning Relevant for Every Student

One of the key elements that make elementary education so effective is the ability to personalize learning. From choice boards to individualized assignments, elementary teachers are masters of tailoring instruction to meet the needs, interests, and abilities of their students. Unfortunately, as students move into middle and high school, personalization often takes a backseat to more rigid, one-size-fits-all teaching approaches. This is a missed opportunity, especially in secondary education, where students are on the verge of becoming independent learners and thinkers.

Personalizing learning in the secondary classroom is not just about giving students choices in what they learn, though that's certainly a part of it. It's about meeting students where they are and providing them with opportunities to engage with the material in ways that resonate with them. It's about creating a classroom environment where every student feels seen, valued, and challenged.

In this chapter, we will explore how personalizing learning can enhance student engagement and achievement in secondary classrooms. We will discuss the importance of knowing your students, using differentiation and choice, and providing opportunities for students to pursue their interests and passions. By the end of this chapter, you'll have practical strategies to create a personalized learning experience that makes every student feel like their education is relevant to them.

The Importance of Knowing Your Students

Personalization begins with knowing your students, not just their academic abilities, but their interests, learning styles, and personal goals. When students feel like their teacher knows and understands them, they are more likely to feel motivated and connected to the content. Getting to know your students isn't just about learning their names or asking about their hobbies; it's about creating an environment where students feel comfortable sharing their thoughts, struggles, and aspirations.

- **Building relationships:** One of the most important steps in personalizing learning is building strong, trusting relationships with students. Take time to learn about each student's interests and strengths. Ask open-ended questions that allow students to express themselves, and actively listen to their responses. This can be done informally through casual conversations or more formally through surveys or one-on-one meetings. When students feel heard and respected, they are more likely to take ownership of their learning and invest in the classroom environment.
- **Understanding learning profiles:** Each student has a unique learning profile, which includes their strengths, weaknesses, and preferred learning styles. Understanding these profiles allows you to better tailor your teaching methods to meet students where they are. For example, some students may learn best through visual aids, while others prefer hands-on activities or group discussions. By recognizing these preferences and adjusting your teaching accordingly, you can create a more inclusive and effective learning experience for everyone.

Differentiating Instruction to Meet Diverse Needs

In a secondary classroom, students come with a wide range of abilities, backgrounds, and learning styles. One of the most effective ways to personalize learning is through differentiation, adapting content, processes, and assessments to meet the needs of all students. Differentiation allows you to provide students with the right level of challenge, support, and enrichment to ensure that they are all able to make progress and succeed.

- **Content differentiation:** Differentiating content means offering students different ways to access the material. For example, in a literature class, you might provide students with texts at varying levels of complexity. Some students may read a shorter, simpler version of the text, while others tackle the full text. You can also offer alternative formats, such as audio or visual versions of a text, to accommodate students with different learning preferences. By providing multiple pathways to the same content, you ensure that all students can engage with the material in a way that is accessible to them.
- **Process differentiation:** Differentiating process involves varying the ways in which students interact with the content. This might include adjusting the pace of lessons, providing additional support through scaffolding, or offering more challenging tasks for advanced learners. For instance, you could offer guided practice for students who need additional support, while allowing others to work independently or in small groups to deepen their understanding. This ensures that every student receives the appropriate level of challenge, without feeling overwhelmed or under-challenged.
- **Product differentiation:** Differentiating product means giving students different ways to demonstrate their learning. Instead of assigning the same project or paper to every student, offer choices that align with students' interests and strengths. Some students may choose to create a presentation, while others might prefer to write a paper, make a video, or design a model. This flexibility allows students to showcase their knowledge in a way that is meaningful to them and taps into their individual talents.

Offering Choice and Voice in Learning

A powerful way to personalize learning is by giving students choice and voice in what they learn and how they demonstrate their understanding. When students have a say in their education, they feel a greater sense of ownership and investment in the process. Choice can take many forms, from letting students pick topics for projects to allowing them to choose the method of assessment that best aligns with their strengths.

- **Choice in topics:** Allowing students to choose topics that interest them can be a highly motivating way to personalize learning. For example, in a history class, you might allow students to choose a particular time period or event to research and present on. In a science class, students could select a topic related to current events, such as climate change or renewable energy. When students are able to explore subjects they are passionate about, they are more likely to engage deeply with the content and produce high-quality work.
- **Choice in learning methods:** In addition to giving students choices in what they learn, it's also important to offer them choices in how they learn. Some students may prefer to work independently, while others thrive in collaborative group settings. By offering different learning formats, such as individual projects, group discussions, or online modules, you can cater to students' varying preferences and create a more inclusive classroom environment.
- **Voice in assessments:** Traditional assessments often leave little room for student input, but personalized assessments allow students to demonstrate their knowledge in ways that reflect their learning styles. For example, instead of relying solely on written tests, consider offering alternative assessments such as presentations, creative projects, or

performance-based tasks. Allowing students to have a voice in how they are assessed not only increases engagement but also gives them a sense of autonomy and pride in their work.

Creating a Relevant and Meaningful Learning Experience

Personalization also involves making learning relevant to students' lives. When students see how the content connects to their interests, goals, and the real world, they are more likely to be engaged and motivated. In secondary education, students are at a critical point where they are thinking about their future careers, personal goals, and the world around them. By connecting classroom learning to these real-world applications, you can make the material feel more meaningful and applicable to their lives.

- **Connecting to personal goals:** Help students make connections between what they are learning in the classroom and their personal aspirations. For example, in a math class, you might show students how the concepts they are learning are used in fields like engineering, architecture, or finance. In a language arts class, you could discuss how strong writing skills are essential for careers in journalism, law, or marketing. When students see how the content will help them achieve their goals, they are more likely to see its value and engage with it more fully.
- **Real-world relevance:** Incorporating real-world applications into lessons can help students see the practical use of what they are learning. Consider using case studies, current events, or simulations that mirror real-world challenges. This approach not only helps students see the relevance of their education but also prepares them for the skills they will need in their future careers.

Empowering Students Through Personalization

At its core, personalization empowers students to take control of their learning. When students feel that their education is tailored to their needs, interests, and strengths, they are more likely to engage in the process and strive for success. Personalization fosters a sense of ownership and responsibility, encouraging students to set goals, monitor their progress, and actively participate in their own growth.

Personalizing learning in secondary classrooms is not about making things easier for students, it's about making learning more accessible, relevant, and meaningful. It's about providing students with the tools and opportunities they need to succeed on their own terms. By getting to know your students, differentiating instruction, offering choice, and connecting learning to the real world, you can create a classroom where every student feels valued, supported, and challenged.

You try it!: Offer students a range of learning options that align with their personal interests and learning styles. For example, when assigning reading material, allow students to choose from a list of books that cater to different genres and interests. You can also provide various project formats, such as written reports, art-based projects, or multimedia presentations, allowing students to demonstrate their understanding in ways that appeal to them.

Chapter 4: From Lecture to Interaction – Creating Active Learning Spaces

In many secondary classrooms, the traditional lecture format still dominates instruction. Teachers stand at the front of the room, delivering content while students sit passively, taking notes or listening quietly. While this model has its place, it does not fully engage students or encourage the kinds of skills that are necessary for success in today's world. In fact, research consistently shows that active learning, where students are actively involved in the learning process, is far more effective at promoting deeper understanding, critical thinking, and retention of knowledge.

Active learning strategies are about shifting the focus from the teacher as the primary source of information to the students as active participants in their own learning. When students are given opportunities to interact with the material, collaborate with peers, and apply what they are learning in real-world contexts, they become more engaged and invested in the process. In this chapter, we will explore how to transform a traditional lecture-based classroom into an interactive, student-centered learning environment.

The Power of Interaction in the Classroom

Active learning is built on the premise that students learn best when they are actively involved in the learning process. When students are merely passive listeners, they are less likely to retain information or develop a deep understanding of the material. However, when students are given the chance to engage with content in hands-on ways, they not only retain more information but also develop the critical thinking and problem-solving skills that are essential for success in the real world.

- **Engagement through interaction:** Interaction allows students to make connections between the new content they

are learning and their prior knowledge or experiences. This connection helps solidify understanding and make the learning more meaningful. For example, when students are asked to discuss a concept in a group or solve a problem together, they are actively processing the information and making it their own. The act of explaining, questioning, and debating enhances their understanding and helps them internalize what they are learning.
- **Collaborative learning:** Interaction often occurs in the form of collaboration. Working in groups allows students to share ideas, solve problems, and learn from one another. Collaborative learning not only deepens students' understanding of the content but also helps them develop valuable social and communication skills. Whether through group discussions, peer teaching, or collaborative projects, students benefit from hearing different perspectives and engaging in conversations that challenge their thinking.

Creating an Interactive Learning Environment

To move from a lecture-based model to one focused on active learning, the classroom environment itself must be designed to encourage interaction. This involves more than simply giving students a few opportunities to discuss the material during class. It requires creating a culture of interaction where students are encouraged to participate, collaborate, and engage with the content in meaningful ways.

- **Flexible seating arrangements:** Traditional rows of desks facing the front can create a passive learning environment. In contrast, flexible seating arrangements allow students to work together, collaborate, and engage more actively with the material. Group seating, for example, fosters discussion and cooperative learning. Students can easily turn to one

another to ask questions, offer opinions, and work together on tasks. By making your classroom seating adaptable, you encourage movement, collaboration, and communication among students.
- **Interactive technology:** Technology can play a significant role in creating an interactive learning space. Tools such as interactive whiteboards, online discussion platforms, and collaborative apps can facilitate student engagement and participation. For example, using digital tools to create interactive quizzes, surveys, or polls allows students to actively participate in the lesson. Online discussion forums or collaborative documents enable students to work together on projects and share their ideas in real time.
- **Student-centered activities:** To promote interaction, it's important to design activities that place the students at the center of the learning process. Instead of simply delivering content through lectures or reading assignments, create opportunities for students to interact with the material. This can include activities such as think-pair-share, case studies, role-playing, or problem-solving tasks. These activities require students to think critically, communicate effectively, and collaborate with others.

Incorporating Real-World Applications

Active learning is not just about classroom activities, it's also about making the content relevant to students' lives. When students can see how the material connects to the real world, they are more likely to engage with it. Real-world applications provide students with opportunities to apply what they are learning to practical, real-life situations, which helps them understand the relevance and importance of their education.

- **Problem-based learning:** One effective strategy for making learning interactive and relevant is problem-based learning (PBL). PBL involves presenting students with real-world problems that they must work together to solve. This approach encourages students to think critically, apply their knowledge, and collaborate with peers. For example, in a science class, students might work together to design an experiment to solve a real-world environmental issue. In a history class, they might investigate the causes and effects of a historical event to draw conclusions about its impact on the present day.
- **Case studies and simulations:** Case studies and simulations are another way to bring real-world applications into the classroom. Case studies present students with detailed scenarios based on actual events or problems, and students must analyze the situation, identify key issues, and propose solutions. Simulations, whether in business, law, or science, allow students to step into real-world roles and experience the challenges and decisions professionals face in their fields. Both case studies and simulations provide students with a hands-on learning experience that is engaging and relevant.

Strategies for Effective Active Learning

Transitioning to an active learning environment requires thoughtful planning and intentional strategies. To ensure that active learning is successful, it's important to choose activities that align with your lesson goals and objectives. Here are some strategies for making active learning work in your classroom:

- **Structured group work:** Group work is a powerful tool for fostering interaction and collaboration, but it needs to be structured effectively. Assign specific roles within the group, such as a facilitator, timekeeper, or recorder, to ensure that

every student is engaged and contributing. Provide clear guidelines for the task at hand, and make sure students have a specific goal or product to work toward.
- **Think-pair-share:** Think-pair-share is a simple but effective active learning strategy that promotes individual reflection and group discussion. First, ask students to think about a question or topic on their own. Then, have them pair up with a partner to discuss their thoughts. Finally, ask pairs to share their ideas with the whole class. This strategy encourages all students to participate and provides opportunities for students to hear different perspectives.
- **Flipped classrooms:** A flipped classroom is an instructional model where students engage with content outside of class (often through video lectures or reading assignments) and use class time for interactive activities. This model allows students to take control of their learning and spend more time applying their knowledge through discussions, problem-solving tasks, and collaborative projects.

The Benefits of Active Learning

The benefits of active learning go far beyond student engagement. When students are actively involved in their learning, they are more likely to retain information, develop critical thinking skills, and become lifelong learners. Active learning also helps students build the skills they will need in the real world, such as teamwork, communication, and problem-solving.

By creating an interactive learning environment, you are setting your students up for success, not only in the classroom but also in their future careers. The skills developed through active learning are the same skills that employers look for: the ability to work collaboratively, think critically, and apply knowledge in practical situations.

By transforming your classroom into a space that values interaction and student-centered learning, you can create an environment where students feel invested in their education and motivated to succeed. Active learning is more than just a teaching method; it's a way to empower students to take ownership of their learning and develop the skills they need to thrive in the classroom and beyond.

You try it!: Replace or supplement traditional lectures with active learning strategies. For example, implement group work, problem-solving activities, or learning stations where students can physically manipulate objects, work through case studies, or engage in project-based learning. This hands-on approach helps students learn by doing rather than passively listening.

Chapter 5: Classroom Management in Secondary Classrooms – Structuring Success through Engagement and Consistency

Managing a secondary level classroom is often one of the greatest challenges educators face. Unlike elementary classrooms, secondary students are navigating adolescence, seeking independence, and testing boundaries, yet they still require structure, support, and guidance to thrive. While many secondary classrooms rely on strict rules and reactive discipline, there is much that can be learned from elementary classroom management strategies. Elementary teachers balance high expectations with engaging routines, clear expectations, and proactive strategies to maintain order. When these strategies are adapted for older students, they can create classrooms that are both structured and dynamic, fostering engagement and learning.

Planning for a Well-Managed Classroom

Effective classroom management begins long before students enter the room. Planning ensures that instruction runs smoothly and minimizes downtime, which is often when behavior issues arise. Key elements include:

- Lesson Flow: Plan lessons with clear transitions, structured activities, and opportunities for movement or engagement to prevent boredom or off-task behavior.

- Materials and Resources: Prepare manipulatives, visuals, technology, and handouts ahead of time. Having materials ready ensures smooth transitions and reduces opportunities for distraction.

- Seating Arrangement: Organize the classroom to promote collaboration while maintaining teacher visibility. Flexible seating can encourage interaction, but clusters or groupings should allow the teacher to monitor student behavior easily.

Creating a Positive and Functional Environment

The classroom environment sets the tone for student behavior. In secondary school, this includes both physical space and emotional climate:

- Classroom Layout: Ensure students can see the board, resources, and each other for group work. Include spaces for collaborative work and independent tasks.
- Visual Cues: Use charts, posters, and anchor charts to remind students of routines, expectations, and learning objectives.
- Classroom Culture: Foster a sense of community where students feel respected, valued, and responsible for their learning. Recognize positive behaviors and celebrate successes to reinforce a culture of accountability.

Attention Grabbers and Transitions

Secondary students often need clear signals to shift focus or transition between activities:

- Non-Verbal Signals: Use hand signals, timers, or lights to indicate transitions or regain attention.
- Verbal Prompts: Short, consistent phrases such as "Eyes up front" or "All set?" help establish routines and clarity.

- Movement Breaks: Incorporate short brain breaks or physical movement, especially after long periods of instruction, to re-engage students and prevent fatigue.

Setting Expectations and Routines

Clarity and consistency are central to successful classroom management:

- Establish Clear Rules: Define and display 3–5 non-negotiable expectations, such as respect, participation, and responsibility.
- Model Behavior: Demonstrate routines, expectations, and procedures explicitly at the start of the year or semester.
- Practice and Reinforce: Give students opportunities to practice routines, transitions, and procedures. Reinforce correct behavior immediately and consistently.
- Student Involvement: Include students in setting classroom norms to increase buy-in and ownership.

Discipline and Redirection

Discipline should be proactive, fair, and constructive rather than punitive:

- Proactive Strategies: Prevent behavior issues through engaging lessons, clear instructions, and consistent monitoring.
- Positive Reinforcement: Recognize students for following expectations, completing tasks, or demonstrating leadership. Examples include verbal praise, "Classroom Bucks," or recognition boards.

- Consistent Consequences: Apply fair, predictable consequences for misbehavior. Keep consequences logical, connected to the misbehavior, and proportional.
- Private Interventions: Address behavioral concerns privately when possible to maintain student dignity and minimize disruption.

Using Elementary Strategies to Support Management

Many strategies from elementary classrooms can be adapted for secondary school:

- Routines and Predictability: Secondary students respond well to predictable routines, including bell schedules, transitions, and structured group activities.
- Visual Reminders: Anchor charts or posters can display class norms, step-by-step procedures, and expectations.
- Active Engagement: Students who are engaged in meaningful learning are less likely to act out. Interactive lessons, collaborative projects, and problem-based learning reduce behavioral challenges.
- Celebrating Success: Recognition systems, shout-outs, and displays of student work foster positive behavior and encourage accountability.

Practical Application: Setting Up Your High School Classroom for Success

1. Plan Ahead: Map out each day's lessons, materials, and transitions. Include backup activities for downtime.

2. Organize the Space: Arrange desks for visibility, collaboration, and accessibility to materials. Include areas for group work and independent study.
3. Establish Norms: Work with students to define rules and expectations. Post them visibly and review them regularly.
4. Use Signals and Attention Grabbers: Establish clear verbal and non-verbal cues to manage transitions and redirect focus.
5. Incorporate Elementary Strategies: Use visual cues, anchor charts, and recognition systems to maintain engagement and reinforce positive behaviors.
6. Monitor and Adjust: Continuously assess classroom dynamics, student engagement, and routines. Adjust procedures as needed to maintain a positive, productive learning environment.

Anecdotal Story

When I moved from elementary schools to working in a middle and high school, I noticed that students often seemed disengaged and distracted during transitions. I supported teachers in implementing routines inspired by my elementary experience: visual schedules, hand signals to regain attention, and recognition charts for positive behavior. Within weeks, students were transitioning smoothly, following expectations, and participating more actively in lessons. What worked in elementary classrooms, consistency, clear expectations, and recognition, was equally powerful in a secondary school setting when adapted thoughtfully.

Chapter 6: Manipulatives, Anchor Charts, and Other Tools for Understanding at Any Age

In elementary classrooms, manipulatives and anchor charts are essential tools that help students interact with and understand complex concepts. These resources allow students to explore ideas hands-on and visually, making learning both engaging and effective. However, as students progress into middle and high school, these tools are often dismissed, with the belief that older students no longer need them. This perception is misleading. Secondary students can still benefit from manipulatives, anchor charts, and several other tools that enhance understanding and promote deeper learning.

In this chapter, we will explore how manipulatives, anchor charts, and other visual and hands-on tools can transform secondary classrooms. These resources are not only valuable for younger learners, they can be powerful assets in middle and high school education, supporting students in grasping complex concepts and engaging more fully with the content. By incorporating a variety of tools, we can create a dynamic learning environment that helps students interact with the material, organize their thoughts, and retain key information.

The Role of Manipulatives in Secondary Education

Manipulatives are physical objects that students use to explore abstract concepts, often making them more accessible and understandable. While manipulatives are commonly used in elementary classrooms, their value extends to secondary education as well. In subjects like math, science, and even social studies, manipulatives allow students to engage with content in hands-on ways that deepen their understanding.

- **Math and Science Manipulatives:** In secondary math classrooms, manipulatives can help students visualize and interact with abstract concepts such as algebraic equations or geometric shapes. For example, algebra tiles can be used to visually represent equations, helping students understand the relationships between terms and variables. In science, 3D models of molecules or chemical structures make it easier for students to grasp complex concepts like molecular bonding or cellular processes. These hands-on tools allow students to move beyond theoretical knowledge and see how concepts work in practice.

- **Real-World Applications:** Manipulatives also offer opportunities for students to connect what they are learning to real-world scenarios. For example, in a business class, students could use play money to simulate market transactions, or in an economics class, students might use different types of currency to model financial exchanges. This practical application reinforces the content and helps students understand how concepts are used outside the classroom.

- **Fostering Engagement and Motivation:** Manipulatives actively engage students by allowing them to interact with the material in a tangible way. When students manipulate objects, they are more likely to retain the information because they are actively involved in the learning process. These tools offer students a more enjoyable and memorable way to learn, which can motivate them to take an active role in their education.

Anchor Charts – Visual Tools for Organizing and Reinforcing Knowledge

Anchor charts are visual displays that summarize key concepts, strategies, or processes. These charts serve as a reference for students, helping them organize their thinking and understand complex ideas. While anchor charts are often associated with elementary classrooms, they are just as beneficial for secondary students.

- **Organizing Complex Information:** In secondary classrooms, anchor charts can simplify complex ideas by visually representing them in a way that is easy to understand. For example, a history teacher might create an anchor chart that outlines the causes and effects of a historical event, helping students see the relationships between different factors. A science teacher could use an anchor chart to illustrate the steps of a scientific experiment or the processes in a biological system. These charts help students break down complicated concepts into manageable pieces.
- **Guiding Problem-Solving and Critical Thinking:** Anchor charts can also serve as guides for critical thinking and problem-solving. For instance, a math teacher might create a chart that outlines the steps involved in solving equations, providing students with a reference that can help them work through problems independently. In an English class, an anchor chart could list strategies for analyzing a piece of literature, helping students develop a more structured approach to interpretation.
- **Collaborative Learning:** Anchor charts are often created with input from students, making them collaborative learning tools. By involving students in the creation of anchor charts, teachers encourage engagement and ownership of the learning process. These charts serve as visual reminders of the class's shared understanding, reinforcing the idea that learning is a collective experience.

Other Tools to Enhance Understanding and Engagement

While manipulatives and anchor charts are powerful tools, there are many other resources that can support student learning in secondary classrooms. Each tool has its own unique way of helping students engage with content and organize their thinking.

- **Graphic Organizers:** Graphic organizers, such as mind maps, Venn diagrams, and T-charts, help students organize and synthesize information visually. These tools are particularly useful for breaking down complex ideas and showing how different concepts relate to one another. For example, a Venn diagram might help students compare and contrast two literary themes, while a mind map could help students brainstorm ideas for a writing assignment. These visual tools give students a clear framework for organizing their thoughts and understanding key concepts.
- **Concept Maps:** Concept maps are another form of visual tool that shows the relationships between different concepts. These maps help students organize information in a way that highlights how different ideas are connected. For instance, in a biology class, a concept map might show how different systems in the body work together, allowing students to see the big picture and how smaller concepts fit into a larger context.
- **Interactive Whiteboards and Technology:** Interactive whiteboards (or smartboards) allow teachers and students to engage with content in dynamic ways. These boards let students move objects, solve problems interactively, and collaborate with their peers. Digital tools like Padlet can also create virtual collaborative spaces, where students can share ideas and build knowledge together. Technology allows for a more interactive and engaging learning experience,

encouraging students to participate and collaborate in ways that traditional methods may not.
- **Interactive Notebooks:** Interactive notebooks are a great way for students to actively engage with content and reflect on their learning. These notebooks can include diagrams, summaries, reflections, and questions, allowing students to personalize their learning experience. As students add to their notebooks over time, they create a valuable resource that they can refer back to when studying or reviewing key concepts.
- **Real-World Objects and Models:** Using real-world objects or models can bring learning to life and help students make connections between abstract concepts and the world around them. For example, in a geography class, students might use a globe or map to explore geographical features, while in a physics class, they might manipulate a model of a car to better understand motion and forces. These tangible resources help students visualize and understand difficult concepts.
- **Digital Tools for Student-Created Content:** Platforms like Canva, Google Slides, or Flipgrid allow students to create their own digital content, such as infographics, presentations, or video reflections. These tools not only help students synthesize information in a creative way but also foster critical thinking and digital literacy.

Why These Tools Matter

Manipulatives, anchor charts, graphic organizers, interactive tools, and real-world objects are not just for elementary students, they are essential resources for secondary classrooms as well. These tools offer multiple ways for students to engage with content, making complex concepts more accessible and enhancing their overall understanding. By incorporating these tools into your classroom, you create an environment where students actively participate in their learning and are more likely to retain the information they encounter.

These tools also foster engagement, which leads to greater motivation and a deeper connection with the material. When students interact with the content in multiple ways, whether through physical manipulatives, visual organizers, or digital tools, they develop a more comprehensive understanding of the material. The combination of visual, hands-on, and digital resources allows students to engage with content in ways that best suit their learning styles and preferences.

Incorporating these tools into your teaching strategies helps create a classroom that values interaction, engagement, and personalized learning. When students feel actively involved in the learning process, they are more likely to succeed, and more importantly, they develop the skills needed to thrive both in school and in the real world.

You try it!: Use manipulatives and hands-on tools to make abstract concepts more concrete. In subjects like math and science, provide students with tools like fraction tiles, models, or interactive digital apps to visualize concepts. You can also create anchor charts with visual steps or diagrams that students can refer to during lessons.

Chapter 7: Vocabulary Walls and Word Walls – Building Language at Every Level

One of the most powerful tools for deepening understanding and promoting academic success is vocabulary development. In secondary classrooms, students are often expected to grasp complex and specialized terms across different subjects, from math and science to history and literature. Without a strong foundation in the language of their respective subjects, students may struggle to fully engage with the material. This is where vocabulary walls and word walls come into play. These tools, which are common in elementary classrooms, are just as essential in middle and high school education.

Vocabulary walls and word walls are visual resources that display key terms and concepts for students to reference. They help reinforce important language and ideas in a way that is interactive, accessible, and ongoing. In this chapter, we will explore how to use vocabulary and word walls effectively in secondary classrooms, the benefits they provide for students, and how they can be adapted to suit the diverse needs of learners at any grade level.

The Power of Vocabulary in Secondary Education

Vocabulary is more than just a set of words; it is the key to understanding content and ideas. In secondary classrooms, students encounter more advanced vocabulary, whether in literature, math, science, or social studies. The language of each subject is unique, and mastering these specialized terms is crucial for academic success.

- **Academic vocabulary:** Academic vocabulary refers to the words and phrases that students need to know in order to engage with academic content. These words often appear across disciplines and include terms such as "analyze," "interpret," "hypothesis," and "compare." These words form the foundation of students' ability to engage in higher-order thinking, express ideas clearly, and understand complex texts.

- **Subject-specific vocabulary:** In addition to academic vocabulary, each subject has its own specialized terminology. For example, in history, terms like "revolution," "imperialism," and "colonialism" are essential to understanding the events and ideas being discussed. In science, words such as "photosynthesis," "cellular respiration," and "molecule" are critical to mastering the content. By building a solid understanding of these subject-specific terms, students can more easily comprehend and apply the material they are learning.
- **Language development across disciplines:** Vocabulary development is essential in all subjects because it is deeply tied to the process of learning and critical thinking. A student who has a strong vocabulary is better able to understand complex concepts, follow instructions, and communicate their thoughts clearly. This helps students in both their academic work and in their ability to collaborate, solve problems, and think critically about the material.

Building a Vocabulary Wall in the Secondary Classroom

A vocabulary wall is a visual tool that displays key vocabulary words related to a specific unit or topic. It can be a central resource in the classroom, constantly updated and referred to as students progress through the content. For secondary classrooms, vocabulary walls can be adapted to meet the needs of different subjects and provide students with easy access to important terms and definitions.

- **Subject-specific vocabulary walls:** For each subject, create a dedicated vocabulary wall that showcases the key terms students need to know. In a science classroom, the vocabulary wall might display terms like "ecosystem," "energy transfer," and "cell division." In a literature class, it could include literary terms like "metaphor," "theme," and "characterization." As students encounter new terms, they can add them to the wall, making it a living resource that grows with the unit.

- **Interactive vocabulary walls:** To make the vocabulary wall more interactive, consider incorporating activities that allow students to engage with the words. For example, students can work in pairs or small groups to create visual representations of the terms, write example sentences, or perform role plays using the words. This active engagement helps students internalize the terms and better understand their meanings.
- **Digital vocabulary walls:** In addition to physical vocabulary walls, digital tools like Padlet can be used to create virtual vocabulary walls. This allows students to contribute terms, definitions, and examples in real time, creating a collaborative online space for learning. Digital vocabulary walls are also easily accessible for students who are learning remotely or need additional support.

The Role of Word Walls in Secondary Classrooms

Word walls, which display words in alphabetical order, serve as a valuable reference for students across subjects. These walls can be used to reinforce key vocabulary and concepts, providing students with a constant visual reminder of the language they are learning.

- **General word walls:** In addition to subject-specific vocabulary walls, a general word wall can be created to highlight common academic words that appear across disciplines. For example, words like "explain," "summarize," "compare," and "analyze" are used in a wide variety of subjects and are crucial for academic success. Having these words prominently displayed in the classroom gives students a resource they can refer to as they engage with content in different subjects.

- **Tiered word walls:** Consider creating tiered word walls that differentiate the difficulty of the vocabulary. For example, tier one words could focus on basic, everyday terms, tier two could include academic words, and tier three might contain subject-specific terms. This allows students to gradually build their vocabulary and expand their understanding as they move from basic to more complex words.
- **Interactive word walls:** Make your word walls interactive by encouraging students to contribute to them. For example, you could have students define words in their own words or create visual cues that represent the meaning of a term. Interactive word walls encourage students to take ownership of their learning and provide opportunities for them to actively engage with the material.

Benefits of Vocabulary and Word Walls in Secondary Classrooms

The use of vocabulary and word walls in secondary classrooms offers numerous benefits for both students and teachers. These tools help students expand their language skills, build connections between concepts, and support their academic growth in a variety of ways.

- **Reinforcing language retention:** The constant exposure to vocabulary words on a wall helps reinforce their meanings and usage. This repeated exposure, combined with the opportunity for students to interact with the words, supports long-term retention and understanding.
- **Supporting struggling readers:** Vocabulary and word walls are particularly helpful for struggling readers, as they provide

visual cues and definitions that aid comprehension. These tools make abstract concepts more concrete and offer additional support for students who may have difficulty processing information through text alone.
- **Encouraging independent learning:** Vocabulary walls encourage students to take responsibility for their own learning. By referring to the wall when they come across unfamiliar terms, students develop independent learning habits and become more confident in their ability to understand complex material.
- **Fostering a language-rich environment:** Both vocabulary and word walls contribute to creating a language-rich environment in the classroom, where students are constantly surrounded by new language and ideas. This environment fosters a culture of learning and academic growth, where students are encouraged to engage with and master the language of their subjects.

Incorporating Vocabulary and Word Walls into Daily Instruction

To make the most of vocabulary and word walls, it is important to incorporate them into daily instruction. Use these tools as an active part of your teaching strategy, engaging students with them regularly and encouraging them to refer to the walls as they work.

- **Daily vocabulary reviews:** At the beginning of each class, take a few minutes to review the vocabulary on the wall. This can be done through quick activities like "word of the day" or by asking students to use the words in a sentence. Regular review helps reinforce the language and ensures that students continue to engage with it.
- **Vocabulary-based activities:** Incorporate vocabulary-based activities into your lessons, such as word sorting, vocabulary

games, or group discussions. These activities give students opportunities to use the words in context and deepen their understanding of their meanings.
- **Assessing vocabulary understanding:** Use formative assessments to check students' understanding of the vocabulary words. This can include vocabulary quizzes, written reflections, or group projects that require students to use the words in meaningful ways.

Vocabulary and word walls are powerful tools that can support student learning in secondary classrooms. By providing students with visual references, interactive opportunities, and consistent exposure to key terms, these tools help students build a strong academic vocabulary and deepen their understanding of complex content. Whether through subject-specific vocabulary walls, general word walls, or interactive activities, these resources encourage students to engage with language in ways that promote long-term learning and academic success.

You try it!: Create a **word wall** in your classroom and encourage students to actively contribute by adding new terms as they learn them. You can use the word wall to support vocabulary development in all subjects, including science, history, and English. Consider using digital tools like Padlet for creating interactive word walls that students can engage with online.

Chapter 8: The Power of Grouped Seating – Collaborative Learning in Secondary Classrooms

Classrooms have traditionally been arranged with desks in rows, all facing the front, where the teacher delivers information. While this layout has its advantages, particularly in maintaining control and focus, it limits student interaction and collaboration. For years, secondary classrooms have maintained this structure, under the assumption that older students no longer need the same kind of social learning that younger students enjoy. However, research shows that collaboration and interaction among students are key to deeper learning, problem-solving, and engagement. Grouped seating arrangements can help transform the classroom into a space that values collaboration, critical thinking, and community.

In this chapter, we will explore the benefits of grouped seating and how it can be implemented in secondary classrooms. We will discuss how collaborative seating arrangements can foster engagement, enhance communication skills, and improve overall student success. Grouped seating allows students to actively participate in their learning, work together to solve problems, and share diverse ideas. We will also look at practical strategies for arranging your classroom to encourage interaction and collaboration, ensuring that every student has the opportunity to contribute.

Why Grouped Seating Matters in Secondary Classrooms

Secondary education often focuses on individual learning, with students being expected to work on assignments independently and quietly. However, one of the most important skills students need to develop is the ability to work with others. Collaborative skills, such as communication, negotiation, and teamwork, are essential in both higher education and the workforce. Grouped seating not only provides students with the opportunity to engage in these skills but also creates a dynamic learning environment that is more engaging and inclusive.

- **Encouraging communication and teamwork:** When students sit in groups, they are more likely to engage in discussions, ask questions, and collaborate on ideas. This interaction enhances learning by allowing students to share their thoughts, challenge each other's thinking, and support each other in problem-solving. By discussing content with peers, students deepen their understanding of the material and learn to communicate their ideas more effectively.
- **Building a sense of community:** Grouped seating fosters a sense of community within the classroom. When students work together, they become part of a learning community where they share responsibility for their collective success. This sense of belonging can increase students' motivation to participate and engage with the content. It also helps create a positive, supportive classroom culture where students feel valued and respected by their peers.
- **Active engagement and responsibility:** In a traditional lecture-style classroom, students may passively absorb information, but in a collaborative seating arrangement, students are actively engaged in the learning process. Group work encourages students to take responsibility for their own learning and the learning of their peers. They become more invested in the material and are more likely to engage with it in meaningful ways.

Benefits of Collaborative Learning Through Grouped Seating

The benefits of collaborative learning extend far beyond academic achievement. When students work together, they develop skills that are essential for success in the modern world. Grouped seating provides an excellent opportunity for students to engage in cooperative learning and build the following skills:

- **Critical thinking:** Working in groups requires students to analyze information, synthesize ideas, and problem-solve together. These skills are crucial in developing the ability to think critically and approach problems from multiple perspectives. Group work encourages students to consider other viewpoints, ask probing questions, and collaboratively come up with solutions.
- **Conflict resolution and negotiation:** Working in groups can sometimes lead to disagreements or differences of opinion. However, this is a valuable learning experience that helps students develop conflict resolution skills. By negotiating with peers and finding compromises, students build interpersonal skills that are crucial for success in school, work, and life.
- **Social skills and empathy:** Grouped seating gives students the opportunity to practice social skills, such as listening, speaking, and collaborating. It also encourages empathy, as students learn to consider and appreciate the perspectives and ideas of their peers. In a diverse classroom, this empathy can foster inclusivity and respect among students from different backgrounds.
- **Motivation and accountability:** When students are working together, they are more likely to stay engaged and motivated to complete tasks. The responsibility to contribute to a group's success encourages accountability. Students are often more motivated to do their best when they know their peers depend on them, and they may be more willing to take risks or challenge their own thinking in the process.

Implementing Grouped Seating in Secondary Classrooms

To make the most of grouped seating, it's important to thoughtfully arrange the classroom and plan activities that promote collaboration. Simply putting students in groups and leaving them to work without structure may not yield the desired results. Instead, consider these strategies to ensure that grouped seating fosters meaningful interaction and collaboration:

- **Strategic groupings:** To maximize the effectiveness of group work, carefully consider how you group students. Grouping by ability can help ensure that all students are challenged appropriately, but it's also important to mix students with different strengths. This ensures that each group has a range of skills and perspectives. Consider grouping students based on their interests, learning styles, or personalities, so they can bring different strengths to the group dynamic.
- **Clear expectations and roles:** When students work in groups, it's important to provide clear expectations and guidelines for participation. Assigning roles within the group, such as facilitator, recorder, timekeeper, and presenter, helps ensure that everyone has a responsibility and that the work is distributed evenly. It also encourages accountability, as students know they are expected to contribute in specific ways.
- **Structured activities:** Collaborative seating is most effective when it is paired with structured group activities that encourage students to engage with the content. Consider incorporating group projects, peer reviews, case studies, or problem-solving tasks. These activities should be designed to require input from every group member and facilitate discussion and collaboration.

- **Frequent movement and flexibility:** Grouped seating should allow for flexibility and movement. Students should have the opportunity to switch groups or collaborate with different peers throughout the semester. This not only helps them develop a range of social and collaborative skills but also prevents group dynamics from becoming stagnant.
- **Assessment and feedback:** After group activities, it's important to assess both the group's work and the individual contributions of each student. Provide timely feedback to help students improve their collaborative skills. You might also consider peer assessments, where students evaluate each other's contributions to the group. This feedback encourages reflection and helps students learn how to work more effectively in groups.

Creating a Classroom Culture of Collaboration

To fully benefit from grouped seating, it's important to create a classroom culture that values collaboration and interaction. Encourage an environment where students feel comfortable sharing ideas, asking questions, and working together toward common goals. This culture of collaboration can be cultivated in several ways:

- **Modeling collaborative behaviors:** As the teacher, model the behaviors you want to see in your students. Demonstrate how to engage in respectful discussions, listen to others, and work together toward a solution. Your example will set the tone for how students interact with one another.
- **Celebrating teamwork:** Recognize and celebrate the successes of group work. Highlight the importance of collaboration in both academic and real-world contexts, and praise groups that demonstrate effective teamwork, problem-solving, and communication.

- **Fostering a growth mindset:** Encourage students to view group work as an opportunity for growth rather than something to be avoided. Help them see that collaboration is an essential skill that will benefit them both in school and beyond. Promote a mindset where students are open to learning from their peers and embrace challenges as a chance to improve.

Group seating and collaborative learning are powerful tools that can transform the secondary classroom into a more interactive and engaging environment. By fostering communication, critical thinking, and teamwork, grouped seating helps students develop skills that are essential for success in school, in their future careers, and in their personal lives. Through thoughtful planning and a supportive classroom culture, grouped seating can encourage students to take ownership of their learning, collaborate with their peers, and build the skills they need to thrive in an increasingly interconnected world.

You try it!: Experiment with flexible seating arrangements in your classroom to promote collaboration. Consider grouping desks into clusters or using round tables for group activities. Regularly rotate group members to give students the opportunity to work with different peers and develop a wider range of collaborative skills.

Chapter 9: Read-Alouds – Engaging Minds Across All Ages

In secondary classrooms, read-alouds are often seen as a strategy reserved for younger students. Many teachers may assume that older students no longer need to be read to or that they should be able to read and analyze texts independently. However, read-alouds remain a powerful tool at all grade levels, offering opportunities for engagement, modeling, and deeper comprehension. When done strategically, reading aloud can transform the way students interact with texts, helping them develop critical thinking skills and a greater appreciation for the material.

In this chapter, we will explore the benefits of read-alouds in secondary education and discuss how to implement them effectively in your classroom. From literature and history to science and math, reading aloud can enhance students' understanding, provide access to complex texts, and create a more dynamic and interactive classroom environment.

The Power of Read-Alouds in Secondary Education

While students in secondary classrooms are often expected to read and analyze texts on their own, read-alouds offer a unique opportunity to bring texts to life, clarify complex ideas, and model critical thinking. Read-alouds provide a shared experience where the teacher and students can engage with the text together, discussing key ideas, themes, and vocabulary. This collective engagement promotes deeper comprehension and allows students to access material they may find challenging on their own.

- **Modeling fluency and comprehension:** When you read aloud to students, you have the chance to model fluent reading and comprehension strategies. As you read, you can pause to highlight important passages, discuss the meaning of

unfamiliar words, or ask questions that prompt students to think critically about the text. By modeling these strategies, you show students how to approach a text more deeply, and you provide them with tools they can use when reading independently.
- **Clarifying complex texts:** Secondary students often encounter dense, complex texts that require close reading and analysis. A read-aloud gives students access to these texts in a way that feels less intimidating. By reading together, you can help break down difficult language, clarify confusing passages, and ensure that all students understand the material. This is particularly important for struggling readers, English language learners, or students with diverse learning needs who may need additional support to comprehend complex content.
- **Building vocabulary and language skills:** Read-alouds provide an opportunity to introduce and reinforce academic vocabulary. As you read aloud, you can pause to define and explain unfamiliar terms, offering students a context for understanding the words. Over time, this repeated exposure to new vocabulary helps students expand their language skills and build a stronger academic vocabulary.

Read-Alouds Across Subjects

While read-alouds are commonly associated with literature classes, they can be an effective strategy in any subject area. From history and social studies to science and even math, reading aloud can deepen students' understanding and make complex material more accessible.

- **Literature and English Language Arts:** In literature classes, read-alouds help students experience the text as it was intended to be heard. By reading aloud, you can emphasize tone, pacing, and character voices, helping students better understand the nuances of the story. Read-alouds also encourage students to reflect on the themes, characters, and plot development as they listen, fostering deeper engagement with the material. In addition, read-alouds can be paired with discussion or group activities that encourage students to analyze the text and explore its meaning.

- **History and Social Studies:** In history or social studies classes, read-alouds can bring historical documents, primary sources, or biographies to life. Reading aloud from a historical document, such as the Declaration of Independence, helps students hear the language in context and discuss its significance. You can pause during the reading to analyze key phrases or ask questions about the document's implications, helping students develop a deeper understanding of historical events and ideas.
- **Science:** Science texts, especially those that explain processes or theories, can often be dense and technical. Read-alouds in science classes give students a chance to hear the material in a more digestible way, while also offering the opportunity for discussion and clarification. You can model how to interpret data, read graphs, or analyze scientific language, providing students with the tools they need to approach scientific texts with confidence.
- **Math:** While math is often seen as a subject best taught through problems and calculations, read-alouds can be effective for explaining word problems or conceptual ideas. For example, reading aloud a story problem allows you to emphasize the key mathematical concepts and guide students through the problem-solving process. Read-alouds can also be used to discuss the history of mathematical discoveries, providing context for the concepts being taught.

Strategies for Effective Read-Alouds

To make read-alouds effective in the secondary classroom, it is important to incorporate strategies that maximize student engagement and comprehension. The following tips can help ensure that your read-alouds are meaningful and impactful:

- **Select the right material:** Choose texts that are appropriate for your students' level of understanding and interest. Whether it's a piece of literature, a historical document, or a scientific text, make sure that the material is engaging and thought-provoking. Texts that are too difficult may leave students feeling frustrated, while texts that are too easy may not challenge them enough. Select material that aligns with your instructional goals and is relevant to the unit or lesson.
- **Read with expression and purpose:** When reading aloud, vary your tone, pace, and volume to bring the text to life. Emphasize key words, phrases, or ideas to help students understand their significance. Use expression to convey the emotions or tone of the material, helping students engage more deeply with the content. Reading with purpose also means pausing at strategic points to ask questions, highlight key concepts, or clarify difficult passages.
- **Encourage student participation:** During the read-aloud, encourage students to actively engage with the text. Ask questions before, during, and after reading to prompt discussion and critical thinking. For example, ask students to predict what might happen next, share their thoughts on the meaning of a passage, or reflect on how the text connects to their own experiences. Encourage students to make annotations or jot down notes as they listen, helping them focus on key ideas and vocabulary.
- **Incorporate discussion and activities:** After the read-aloud, engage students in a discussion or activity that reinforces the

content and encourages deeper exploration. This can include small-group discussions, written reflections, or creative projects. By reflecting on the material and discussing it with their peers, students deepen their understanding and make connections between the text and the larger themes or concepts.

Creating a Classroom Culture of Reading

Incorporating read-alouds into your classroom can help foster a culture of reading, where students see the value of engaging with texts in meaningful ways. By modeling a love for reading and demonstrating how to interact with texts, you encourage students to develop their own reading habits and a deeper appreciation for literature and other content areas.

- **Read-aloud as a classroom ritual:** Make read-alouds a regular part of your classroom routine. Set aside time each day or week to read aloud to your students, helping them develop a consistent reading habit. When students know that read-alouds are an integral part of their learning experience, they are more likely to look forward to these sessions and engage with the material.
- **Celebrating diverse voices:** Choose texts that represent a variety of voices, cultures, and perspectives. Read-alouds provide an opportunity to introduce students to authors, historical figures, and cultural stories they may not have encountered before. This fosters inclusivity and broadens students' understanding of the world around them.

Read-alouds are a valuable tool for engaging students, modeling reading strategies, and enhancing comprehension at every grade level. By incorporating read-alouds into your secondary classroom, you help students develop a deeper understanding of complex material, build their vocabulary, and engage in critical thinking. When students hear texts read aloud, they not only access the content in a new way but also experience the joy and excitement of learning through literature, history, and beyond.

You try it!: Incorporate **read-alouds** in various subjects, even in high school. Choose texts that align with your curriculum, whether they are excerpts from novels, historical speeches, or scientific articles. Read aloud with expression, stopping occasionally to ask students questions, model annotation, or make connections to the content.

Chapter 10: Highlighters, Post-Its, and Interactive Notebooks – Creating Tools for Active Learning

In secondary classrooms, where content becomes more advanced and the expectations for students' academic work increase, it's easy for traditional methods of engagement to fade into the background. Teachers often assume that students no longer need to actively engage with texts or materials in a hands-on way. However, tools like highlighters, post-its, and interactive notebooks can be incredibly effective in creating active learning experiences. These tools are not just about making learning more fun, they are powerful resources that help students actively interact with the content, organize their thoughts, and retain important information.

In this chapter, we will explore how to effectively incorporate highlighters, post-its, and interactive notebooks into your classroom. These tools help students actively process information, engage with the material in a deeper way, and take ownership of their learning. Whether it's highlighting key concepts in a text, using post-its for personal reflections or group collaboration, or organizing notes in an interactive notebook, these tools provide students with resources that are both practical and effective in supporting their learning.

The Power of Highlighters in Active Learning

Highlighters are simple yet incredibly effective tools that can help students engage with texts more actively. While students may be used to simply highlighting information, there are strategies for using highlighters that encourage critical thinking, organization, and deeper understanding.

- **Highlighting key concepts and themes:** In a literature class, highlighters can be used to identify key themes, symbols, or

character traits in a novel. For example, students could highlight passages that reveal important aspects of a character's development, making it easier to track changes throughout the text. In a history class, students can use highlighters to emphasize key dates, events, or concepts that are critical to understanding historical processes or trends.
- **Color-coded highlighting for organization:** Highlighters can be even more effective when students use different colors to highlight different types of information. For instance, students could use one color to highlight important dates, another color for key people or events, and a third color for concepts. This color-coded system helps students organize the information visually and allows them to quickly identify relationships between concepts or ideas. By categorizing the material this way, students are able to better comprehend and recall the material when it's time for review or discussion.
- **Highlighting for analysis and questioning:** Highlighters can also be used to encourage deeper analysis. For example, while reading a passage, students can highlight sections that they have questions about or find confusing. Later, in a class discussion, they can bring up these highlighted sections and ask for clarification or offer interpretations. This technique encourages active engagement with the text and promotes critical thinking.

Using Post-Its for Reflection and Collaboration

Post-its are another versatile tool that can encourage active learning in the classroom. They are great for quick notes, personal reflections, and collaborative activities, making them a valuable resource for secondary students.

- **Personal reflections and annotations:** Post-its allow students to jot down their thoughts, questions, or ideas as they read or engage with a lesson. For example, while reading a novel, students can use post-its to write down personal reflections on specific passages, noting how they connect to their own experiences or how they relate to the themes of the text. This practice helps students interact with the material on a deeper level and gives them an opportunity to organize their thoughts before engaging in class discussions.

- **Sticky notes for questioning and engagement:** Post-its can also be used for questioning, which is an essential part of active learning. Students can write questions on post-its as they read, whether they are seeking clarification, exploring alternative interpretations, or trying to make connections to other subjects. These questions can be shared during class discussions, helping students engage with the material more fully and encouraging them to think critically about what they are learning.
- **Collaborative post-it activities:** In group activities, post-its can be a tool for collaboration. For example, after reading a chapter, students could work in groups to create a visual map of key ideas using post-its. Each student could contribute a post-it with a summary of a key point, and the group could arrange the post-its on a board or chart to visually represent the connections between ideas. This collaborative approach encourages teamwork and allows students to see how different pieces of information fit together.

Interactive Notebooks – A Personalized Learning Resource

Interactive notebooks are one of the most dynamic tools for active learning. These notebooks allow students to record, organize, and reflect on their learning in ways that are both engaging and personal. Interactive notebooks are particularly effective because they encourage students to take ownership of their learning process and allow them to create a resource they can refer to throughout the course.

- **Organizing and synthesizing information:** In an interactive notebook, students can organize their notes by topic, concept, or unit. They can include summaries of lessons, diagrams, charts, and even personal reflections. This organization helps students see how different ideas connect and provides them with a comprehensive resource for review and study. Interactive notebooks also give students a way to synthesize the information in their own words, which enhances understanding and retention.
- **Creative engagement with content:** Interactive notebooks are more than just a place for notes. They offer students the opportunity to engage with content creatively. For example, students can create diagrams, charts, or illustrations to represent key concepts or create mind maps to organize ideas. This creative approach helps students think critically about the material and allows them to express their understanding in a way that goes beyond traditional note-taking.
- **Reflection and self-assessment:** Interactive notebooks encourage students to reflect on what they have learned and assess their understanding. After each lesson or unit, students can add a reflection page where they summarize what they found most interesting, what they need more help with, or how the material connects to previous lessons. This reflective process helps students identify gaps in their understanding and provides teachers with insight into students' learning.
- **Personalization of learning:** One of the most powerful aspects of interactive notebooks is that they allow students to personalize their learning. They can add notes, drawings, or additional information that is relevant to them. This personalization helps students feel more connected to the

material and allows them to build a resource that fits their individual learning styles and needs.

Combining Highlighters, Post-Its, and Interactive Notebooks for Active Learning

The true power of these tools is realized when they are used together in a cohesive, interactive learning system. Highlighters, post-its, and interactive notebooks complement each other by allowing students to engage with the material in different ways and reinforce their understanding through multiple avenues.

- **Combining highlighting and interactive notebooks:** Students can use highlighters to mark important ideas in texts, and then transfer these ideas into their interactive notebooks for further exploration. For example, after reading a passage, students can highlight key phrases and then create a mind map or summary in their notebooks to further explain the material. This process reinforces comprehension and helps students internalize what they are learning.
- **Using post-its within interactive notebooks:** Post-its can be incorporated into interactive notebooks to encourage deeper engagement. For example, students might add post-it notes to specific pages in their notebooks where they want to highlight a question or make a personal connection. Post-its can also be used for group activities, where students work together to add comments or reflections on a particular topic in their notebooks.
- **Promoting collaboration and reflection:** By combining all three tools, highlighters, post-its, and interactive notebooks, students are able to engage with the material on multiple levels. They can highlight important concepts, reflect on what they've learned, and collaborate with peers to expand their understanding. This multi-faceted approach creates an

active learning environment where students are engaged, motivated, and encouraged to think critically.

Highlighters, post-its, and interactive notebooks are simple tools, but they have a profound impact on the way students engage with and retain information. By incorporating these tools into your classroom, you provide students with opportunities to actively process and interact with the material, organize their thoughts, and take ownership of their learning. These tools help make the learning process more engaging and personalized, supporting students in becoming independent, reflective learners.

You try it!: Encourage students to use **interactive notebooks** to organize their notes and thoughts. Have students highlight key concepts, annotate their work with post-its, and regularly revisit their notebooks to track progress. This process helps students engage more actively with the material and improve retention.

Chapter 11: Using Data to Inform Instruction

In education, one of the most powerful tools teachers have is data. When used effectively, data can guide instruction, enhance student learning, and improve overall educational outcomes. The challenge, however, is not just in collecting data, but in knowing how to interpret it and use it to make informed decisions that benefit all students. This chapter explores how secondary educators can use data to inform their teaching practices, adapt instruction to meet diverse student needs, and ensure that every student has the opportunity to succeed.

The Importance of Data in Education

Data is not just a set of numbers on a spreadsheet or a score on a test. It provides valuable insights into how students are progressing, where they are excelling, and where they may need additional support. In secondary classrooms, where content becomes more complex and the demands on students increase, data plays an essential role in ensuring that learning is personalized, targeted, and responsive.

- **Tracking student progress:** Data allows teachers to track students' progress over time, identifying patterns and trends in their performance. Whether through formative assessments, class participation, or homework assignments, this data provides a comprehensive view of a student's academic journey. By reviewing trends in student performance, teachers can pinpoint areas where students are struggling and adjust their teaching methods to address those challenges.
- **Personalizing instruction:** Every student learns differently, and data helps teachers identify those individual needs. When teachers use data to guide their decisions, they can create a

more personalized learning experience for each student. For example, a student who is struggling with reading comprehension may benefit from additional support, while a student who excels can be provided with enrichment opportunities. Data ensures that all students receive the appropriate level of challenge and support to thrive in the classroom.

- **Making data-driven decisions:** Using data to inform instruction helps teachers move away from a one-size-fits-all approach. Rather than relying solely on intuition or guesswork, teachers can make decisions based on evidence. This might involve choosing specific instructional strategies, adjusting the pacing of a lesson, or providing targeted interventions to address gaps in understanding. Data-driven decisions lead to more effective teaching practices and greater student success.

Types of Data to Collect

There are several types of data that can be used to inform instruction, each offering unique insights into student performance and progress. These include both quantitative data, such as test scores, and qualitative data, such as observations and student feedback.

- **Formative assessments:** These assessments are conducted throughout the learning process, providing ongoing feedback on student understanding. Formative assessments can take many forms, such as quizzes, exit tickets, peer reviews, and in-class activities. The goal is not to assign a grade, but to gather data on what students know and where they may need additional support. By using formative assessments regularly, teachers can make adjustments to their teaching before students fall behind.

- **Summative assessments:** Summative assessments, such as final exams, end-of-unit tests, or major projects, offer a snapshot of student learning at a specific point in time. While summative assessments provide valuable information about overall performance, they should be used alongside formative assessments to ensure that instruction is responsive and reflective of ongoing progress.
- **Observational data:** Teachers can gather valuable data through observations of student behavior, participation, and engagement. By paying attention to how students interact with the material, each other, and the classroom environment, teachers can gather qualitative data that helps them understand students' needs. Observations are particularly important for gauging engagement and motivation, as well as identifying non-academic challenges that may be affecting learning.
- **Student feedback:** Students' voices should be an integral part of the data collection process. Regular check-ins with students about their learning experiences, through surveys, individual conferences, or open-ended questions, provide important insights into how they feel about the material, what's working, and where they may need more help. By including student feedback in the data-gathering process, teachers can ensure that their instruction is meeting students' needs and preferences.
- **Standardized test data:** While standardized tests are often used for accountability purposes, they also provide valuable insights into student performance. Data from standardized tests can help identify patterns across different student groups, allowing teachers to assess how well students are mastering grade-level content. However, this data should always be viewed in conjunction with other types of data to provide a fuller picture of student learning.

Analyzing and Interpreting Data

Once data is collected, the next step is analyzing it in order to make informed decisions. The goal is to turn raw data into actionable insights that can drive instruction.

- **Identify trends and patterns:** The first step in analyzing data is to look for trends or patterns. Are there areas where most students are excelling, or areas where many students are struggling? For example, if a large group of students is struggling with a particular concept, this may indicate that the instruction or resources provided need to be adjusted. If one student consistently excels in a particular area, it might be time to provide enrichment opportunities.
- **Disaggregate data:** To ensure that all students are receiving the support they need, it's important to disaggregate data by different student groups. For example, you can analyze data by gender, ethnicity, English language proficiency, or special education status. This allows you to identify achievement gaps and target interventions more effectively.
- **Consider student context:** When analyzing data, it's important to consider the broader context. Are there external factors, such as social or emotional challenges, that may be affecting a student's performance? Analyzing data in context helps teachers take a holistic approach to supporting students and ensures that all factors impacting their learning are considered.
- **Track individual progress:** While looking at overall trends is important, it's also crucial to track individual student progress. Use data to track how each student is progressing toward mastery of specific learning objectives. This allows for personalized support, whether that means providing extra help for a struggling student or offering additional challenges for a student who has mastered the material.

Using Data to Adapt Instruction

Once the data has been analyzed, the next step is to adapt instruction based on the insights gained. Data should inform every aspect of teaching, from lesson planning and pacing to groupings and assessments.

- **Adjust the pace of instruction:** If data shows that students are struggling to grasp a particular concept, you may need to slow down and spend more time reinforcing the material. Alternatively, if students are mastering content quickly, you can adjust the pacing to introduce more challenging material or move on to the next concept. Adapting the pace ensures that all students are receiving the appropriate level of challenge.
- **Differentiate instruction:** Data provides teachers with the information needed to differentiate instruction for diverse learners. For example, if data shows that a group of students is struggling with reading comprehension, you may choose to provide additional reading support or modify assignments to make the material more accessible. On the other hand, students who are excelling might benefit from more advanced tasks that push their critical thinking and problem-solving skills.
- **Target interventions:** For students who are struggling, data helps identify which interventions are most appropriate. Whether it's one-on-one tutoring, peer support, or small group instruction, targeted interventions allow you to provide the specific support that each student needs. Data can also help you monitor the effectiveness of these interventions and adjust them as needed.
- **Provide timely feedback:** Data-driven instruction allows teachers to give timely and targeted feedback to students. By using formative assessments and observational data, you can

provide feedback that helps students understand their strengths and areas for growth. When feedback is given in real-time, students have the opportunity to act on it immediately, leading to faster progress.

The Benefits of Data-Driven Instruction

The benefits of using data to inform instruction are clear. By leveraging data, teachers can make more informed decisions, personalize learning, and provide targeted support to all students. Data-driven instruction leads to more effective teaching, greater student engagement, and improved academic outcomes. It allows teachers to be responsive to students' needs and ensures that no student is left behind.

By integrating data into every aspect of teaching, you create a classroom environment that is dynamic, responsive, and focused on student success. Data is not just about numbers, it is a tool for creating a more personalized, engaging, and effective learning experience.

You try it!: Regularly collect formative assessment data (e.g., quizzes, exit tickets) and use it to inform your teaching. Identify areas where students struggle and adjust your instruction accordingly. You can use data-tracking sheets or digital tools like Google Forms to easily collect and analyze student responses.

Chapter 12: Checking for Understanding – Strategies to Gauge Student Learning

In secondary classrooms, ensuring that students grasp the material is a critical aspect of teaching. Simply delivering content is not enough, teachers must consistently check to see whether students understand what is being taught. This process, known as checking for understanding (CFU), helps teachers make real-time adjustments to instruction, identify areas where students are struggling, and provide support before misconceptions become entrenched.

In this chapter, we will explore the importance of checking for understanding in secondary classrooms and discuss a variety of strategies that can be used to assess student comprehension during lessons. By implementing these strategies, teachers can ensure that all students are actively engaged, and they can make adjustments to their teaching to meet the needs of every learner.

Why Checking for Understanding is Essential

Checking for understanding is more than just asking students, "Do you understand?" It involves actively engaging students in the learning process and assessing their comprehension in a variety of ways. This allows teachers to gather data about student progress, identify misunderstandings, and ensure that students are moving forward in their learning journey. Here are a few key reasons why checking for understanding is essential in secondary education:

- **Real-time feedback:** CFU provides immediate feedback on whether students have grasped key concepts. This allows teachers to quickly assess whether the lesson is effective or if adjustments need to be made. Instead of waiting for a quiz or test to find out whether students understood, teachers can use CFU strategies during the lesson to gauge student learning.

- **Preventing misconceptions:** If students don't fully understand a concept, they may develop misconceptions that can hinder their ability to learn more advanced material. By regularly checking for understanding, teachers can catch these misconceptions early and address them before they become more deeply ingrained.
- **Encouraging student engagement:** When students know that they will be regularly checked for understanding, they are more likely to stay engaged in the lesson. CFU strategies often require active participation, which encourages students to pay attention, think critically, and reflect on their learning. This leads to a more dynamic and interactive classroom environment.
- **Adjusting instruction:** Checking for understanding allows teachers to adjust their instruction on the fly. If students are struggling with a concept, the teacher can slow down, reexplain the material, or provide additional support. Alternatively, if students are grasping the material quickly, the teacher can move on to more challenging material or provide enrichment opportunities.

Effective CFU Strategies for Secondary Classrooms

There are numerous strategies teachers can use to check for understanding, each suited to different teaching styles, lesson types, and student needs. Here are some of the most effective methods for assessing student comprehension in real time:

- **Questioning Techniques:**
  One of the most common ways to check for understanding is through questioning. However, not all questions are equally effective. Open-ended questions that encourage students to explain their thinking can provide valuable insights into their understanding. For example, instead of asking, "Do you

understand this concept?" you could ask, "Can you explain why this principle works the way it does?" or "How would you apply this concept in a real-world scenario?" These types of questions encourage students to demonstrate their understanding and articulate their reasoning.

Additionally, using techniques like **wait time**, pausing for a few seconds after asking a question, gives students time to process their thoughts and respond more thoughtfully.

- **Exit Tickets:**

Exit tickets are short prompts that students respond to at the end of a lesson. These prompts can be written or verbal, and they allow teachers to quickly assess whether students have grasped the key concepts. For example, an exit ticket might ask students to summarize what they learned, identify a key takeaway from the lesson, or list any questions they still have. Exit tickets are quick, easy to use, and provide immediate feedback on student comprehension.

Exit tickets can also help identify trends in understanding across the class. If many students are struggling with the same concept, it may signal that further clarification or review is needed.

- **Thumbs Up/Thumbs Down (or Other Quick Visual Indicators):**

For more informal and immediate checks, teachers can use visual indicators such as thumbs up, thumbs down, or other hand signals. After explaining a concept, the teacher can ask students to give a thumbs up if they understand, a thumbs down if they don't, or a thumbs sideways if they are unsure. This allows teachers to gauge comprehension quickly and make adjustments as needed.

- **Peer Teaching and Pair Work:**

One effective way to check for understanding is by having students explain the material to each other. In peer teaching, students pair up and take turns explaining a concept to their partner. If a student can explain the concept clearly to someone else, it demonstrates a solid understanding of the material. This technique encourages active engagement and gives students the opportunity to consolidate their learning through teaching.

Additionally, pair work can provide immediate feedback in a low-pressure environment, allowing students to discuss their thoughts and clarify misunderstandings with a peer before they share with the entire class.

- **Think-Pair-Share:**

Think-Pair-Share is a strategy that encourages students to think individually, discuss their ideas with a partner, and then share with the class. After posing a question or presenting new material, the teacher asks students to think about their response for a moment. Then, students pair up to discuss their thoughts, and finally, they share their answers with the whole class.

This strategy gives students the opportunity to verbalize their understanding, practice speaking in front of others, and receive immediate feedback from both their partner and the teacher. It also allows teachers to check for understanding in a more informal and collaborative way.

- **Quizzes and Polls:**

Short quizzes or polls are excellent tools for checking for understanding, especially when you need data quickly. Technology platforms like Kahoot, Google Forms, or Poll Everywhere allow teachers to conduct quick polls or quizzes that students can complete in real-time. These tools provide immediate feedback on student comprehension, allowing teachers to adjust instruction as needed.

Additionally, quizzes can serve as a formative assessment

tool, helping teachers track student progress over time and identify patterns in areas of difficulty.

Using CFU Data to Inform Instruction

The data gathered from CFU strategies should be used to adjust instruction and guide next steps in teaching. The feedback provides valuable insights into what students understand and where they need more support.

- **Adjusting pacing:**
  If a CFU strategy reveals that students are struggling with a concept, teachers can slow down and spend more time reinforcing the material. Conversely, if students are grasping the content quickly, the teacher can speed up or introduce more challenging material.
- **Differentiating instruction:**
  Data from CFU strategies can help teachers identify students who may need additional support or enrichment. For example, if a student is struggling with a particular concept, the teacher can provide additional resources, offer one-on-one assistance, or create a small group session to address specific needs. On the other hand, if a student excels, the teacher can offer more advanced tasks to further challenge them.
- **Targeting interventions:**
  If many students are struggling with the same concept, it may be necessary to revisit the material, offer additional practice, or explore alternative explanations. CFU data can help pinpoint areas where interventions are needed, allowing for a more targeted approach to addressing learning gaps.

Creating a Classroom Culture of Continuous Feedback

Checking for understanding is not just a tool for teachers, it's a strategy that can help students become more engaged, reflective, and self-aware learners. By making CFU a regular part of classroom practice, teachers create a culture of continuous feedback, where both students and teachers are actively involved in the learning process.

- **Encourage student self-assessment:**
  Encourage students to regularly check their own understanding. This can be done through self-reflection activities, journals, or quizzes. When students assess their own learning, they take ownership of their progress and are better able to identify areas where they need to focus.
- **Promote a growth mindset:**
  By using CFU strategies, teachers can reinforce the idea that learning is an ongoing process, not a fixed outcome. Students who see feedback as a tool for improvement rather than as a judgment of their abilities are more likely to embrace challenges and persist through difficulties.

Checking for understanding is an essential part of effective teaching. By using a variety of strategies to assess student comprehension in real time, teachers can adapt their instruction to meet students' needs, prevent misconceptions, and create an engaging, responsive classroom environment. Ultimately, these strategies help ensure that every student has the opportunity to succeed and thrive in the classroom.

You try it!: Use informal checks for understanding, such as "thumbs up/thumbs down," polls, or exit tickets. This quick feedback will allow you to gauge how well students understand the material, and it gives you the flexibility to adjust your teaching on the spot. You can also use digital tools like Socrative or Kahoot! for real-time assessments.

Chapter 13: Small Group Instruction – Tailoring Learning to Meet Student Needs

In secondary classrooms, one of the most effective ways to differentiate instruction and provide personalized support is through small group instruction. While whole-class lessons are valuable for introducing new content, small group instruction allows teachers to focus on the specific needs of individual students or groups of students. This approach enables teachers to provide targeted support, offer enrichment opportunities, and adjust instruction to meet students where they are in their learning journey.

In this chapter, we will explore the benefits of small group instruction, how to effectively implement it in your classroom, and practical strategies for organizing and managing small group activities. Additionally, we will discuss how small group instruction fits into the **Multi-Tiered System of Supports (MTSS)** framework, where students receive varying levels of intervention based on their individual needs. Whether you are working with struggling learners or providing advanced tasks for high-achieving students, small group instruction can be a powerful tool for fostering deeper understanding and promoting student success.

The Benefits of Small Group Instruction

Small group instruction offers several distinct advantages over traditional whole-class teaching methods. By working with smaller groups of students, teachers can provide more personalized attention, facilitate more in-depth discussions, and target specific learning needs. Here are some of the key benefits of small group instruction:

- **Personalized learning:** One of the biggest advantages of small group instruction is the ability to tailor lessons to the needs of individual students. In a whole-class setting, it's often difficult to address the diverse needs of all students.

Small groups allow you to focus on the specific strengths and weaknesses of the students within the group, providing support where it's needed most. Whether it's offering more challenging material for advanced students or providing additional explanations for struggling students, small group instruction allows you to meet each student's unique needs.
- **Increased student engagement:** In a small group setting, students are more likely to participate in discussions, ask questions, and share their ideas. The smaller group size creates a more comfortable, less intimidating environment for students, allowing them to engage more actively with the content. This increased participation leads to a deeper understanding of the material and promotes critical thinking skills.
- **Opportunities for targeted support:** Small group instruction allows teachers to provide more targeted support to students who may be struggling with specific concepts or skills. Whether it's through one-on-one instruction or group work, small groups offer the opportunity to address individual learning gaps and provide the necessary scaffolding to help students succeed.
- **Collaboration and peer learning:** Small groups foster collaboration among students, encouraging them to work together, share ideas, and learn from one another. Peer teaching and discussion can help students solidify their understanding of concepts, as explaining a concept to others is one of the best ways to reinforce learning. Collaboration also builds communication and teamwork skills, which are essential for success in both academic and real-world contexts.

How to Organize Small Group Instruction

The key to effective small group instruction lies in how you organize the groups and how you structure the activities. Here are several strategies for organizing small group instruction and ensuring that it meets the needs of all students:

- **Flexible grouping:** One of the most effective strategies for small group instruction is flexible grouping, where students are grouped based on their specific needs, interests, or learning profiles. These groups should not be fixed; instead, students can be moved between groups as needed. For example, if a student is struggling with a particular concept, they might be placed in a small group that focuses on that area of weakness. Alternatively, if a student is excelling, they might be placed in a group that explores more advanced content or engages in enrichment activities. Flexible grouping ensures that students receive the right level of challenge and support throughout the learning process.
- **Interest-based grouping:** Another effective way to group students is based on their interests. For example, if you're teaching a unit on social studies, you might group students based on the topics they are most interested in, allowing them to explore specific aspects of history or geography that capture their attention. Interest-based grouping fosters motivation and engagement, as students are more likely to invest in the material when it aligns with their personal interests.
- **Ability-based grouping:** In some cases, it may be beneficial to group students based on their academic abilities. For example, if some students are struggling with reading comprehension, you might create a group that focuses on strengthening reading skills, while more advanced readers work on higher-level tasks. While ability-based grouping is

useful for providing targeted support, it's important to ensure that students are not pigeonholed into a particular group permanently. Rotating groupings can help prevent any negative impact on student self-esteem and keep the learning experience dynamic.
- **Random grouping:** Randomly assigning students to small groups can also be a valuable strategy, especially when the goal is to encourage collaboration, build community, or provide diverse perspectives. Random grouping prevents students from always working with the same peers, fostering new interactions and allowing students to learn from one another in different ways.

Strategies for Effective Small Group Instruction

Once you've organized your groups, it's important to structure your small group activities effectively to maximize student engagement and learning. Here are some strategies that can help ensure the success of small group instruction:

- **Clear expectations and roles:** To ensure that small group activities are productive, it's essential to set clear expectations and assign roles within each group. For example, in a discussion-based group, you might assign one student to be the facilitator, another to be the note-taker, and another to be the timekeeper. By assigning specific roles, you ensure that all students are actively involved in the activity and that the group stays on task.
- **Focused tasks and goals:** Small group activities should have specific goals or tasks that students are working toward. Whether it's solving a math problem, creating a presentation, or discussing a reading, each group should know what they are expected to accomplish by the end of the session. This

focus helps prevent groups from becoming distracted and ensures that they are working towards a clear objective.
- **Differentiated tasks:** Small group instruction provides an excellent opportunity for differentiation. Depending on the needs of the group, you can modify the task to ensure that it is appropriately challenging. For example, if you are working with a group of struggling students, you might provide additional scaffolding, such as graphic organizers or sentence starters. For more advanced groups, you can offer more complex tasks or encourage independent exploration of the topic.
- **Use of formative assessments:** While small group instruction is taking place, it's important to continuously check for understanding. You can use quick formative assessments, such as questioning, polls, or written reflections, to gauge student comprehension and adjust instruction accordingly. These assessments provide valuable insights into whether the students are grasping the material and whether further intervention is needed.
- **Reflection and debriefing:** At the end of a small group session, encourage students to reflect on what they learned and how they contributed to the group. This reflection process helps students internalize the material and reinforces the value of collaboration. You can also debrief with the class as a whole, discussing the key takeaways from each group's work and highlighting important insights.

Managing Small Group Instruction in a Secondary Classroom

One of the biggest challenges with small group instruction is managing the entire classroom while working with individual groups. Here are some strategies to ensure smooth and effective management:

- **Create independent activities for the rest of the class:** While you are working with small groups, the rest of the class should have independent tasks to complete. These tasks should be engaging and purposeful, such as independent reading, individual practice problems, or collaborative tasks that do not require direct teacher supervision. This ensures that students remain productive while you focus on the small groups.
- **Rotate through groups:** As the teacher, you don't need to spend equal amounts of time with each group. Instead, you can rotate through the groups, spending more time with students who need additional support and less time with students who are more independent. By moving between groups, you can monitor progress, provide feedback, and ensure that all students are on track.
- **Set time limits:** To keep small group sessions focused and efficient, set clear time limits for each activity. Give students a set amount of time to complete their tasks and check in regularly to ensure they stay on task. Time limits help prevent groups from getting off track and ensure that all groups have enough time to complete the activity.

Small group instruction is an invaluable tool for secondary educators, allowing them to provide personalized, targeted support to students. Whether you are working with struggling learners, offering enrichment opportunities, or fostering collaboration and peer learning, small group instruction helps meet the diverse needs of students. By organizing groups effectively, setting clear expectations, and using differentiated tasks, you can create an engaging, student-centered learning environment that promotes deeper understanding and academic success.

Incorporating MTSS and Tiered Instruction in Small Group Instruction

One of the most effective frameworks for ensuring that all students receive the right level of support is the Multi-Tiered System of Supports (MTSS). MTSS is a comprehensive, school-wide approach that provides targeted interventions for students based on their needs. It's designed to support the academic, behavioral, and social-emotional growth of all students through tiered levels of intervention.

In the context of small group instruction, MTSS and tiered instruction provide a framework for organizing and delivering interventions and supports to students at varying levels of need. Here's how MTSS and tiered instruction align with small group teaching and how you can integrate these concepts into your classroom.

Understanding the Three Tiers of MTSS

MTSS is based on three tiers of support, each designed to meet the needs of different students. Small group instruction can be a powerful tool for delivering support at each of these tiers.

1. **Tier 1: Universal Support (Core Instruction)**

- **Whole-Class Instruction:** In Tier 1, all students receive high-quality core instruction in the general education classroom. The teacher provides a variety of instructional strategies that meet the diverse needs of students. In this tier, small group instruction can be used to extend or reinforce core lessons for all students. For example, while most of the class is working independently, small groups of students who are excelling can work on more challenging tasks, ensuring they remain engaged.
- **Flexible Grouping:** Tier 1 supports include differentiated small groups based on students' readiness, interests, or learning profiles. In secondary classrooms, this may look like creating flexible groups for collaborative projects or activities that support different learning needs, without focusing on remediation.

2. **Tier 2: Targeted Support (Intervention)**
   - **Targeted Small Groups:** Students who are struggling to meet grade-level expectations may require more focused support. This is where Tier 2 interventions come into play. Small group instruction becomes more targeted, with the teacher working with students who need additional help. For example, students who are struggling with reading comprehension could be grouped together for a targeted, skill-building lesson. These interventions are more specific than Tier 1 instruction and are designed to close learning gaps.
   - **Progress Monitoring:** In Tier 2, it's crucial to monitor students' progress frequently. Teachers can use formative assessments, quizzes, or progress check-ins to track how students are responding to the

interventions. Small group instruction allows teachers to give immediate feedback and adjust the interventions based on students' progress.

3. **Tier 3: Intensive Support (Individualized Intervention)**
   - **Intensive Small Groups or One-on-One Instruction:** Tier 3 involves the most intensive support for students who continue to struggle despite Tier 1 and Tier 2 interventions. Small group instruction in Tier 3 is highly focused and individualized. For example, students who are significantly behind in reading may need small groups focused solely on phonics, fluency, or comprehension. Some students may require one-on-one support to meet their individual needs, allowing the teacher to provide the level of attention and tailored instruction necessary for success.
   - **Individualized Learning Plans:** At this tier, it's important to have a clear plan for each student's learning, which is based on data from assessments, observations, and previous interventions. Small group instruction can help deliver this tailored instruction effectively, ensuring that each student receives the precise support they need.

Small Group Instruction in the MTSS Framework

Small group instruction plays a key role in the MTSS framework. It allows for instruction that is responsive to students' needs, whether they are in Tier 1, Tier 2, or Tier 3. By using small groups at each tier, teachers can provide more personalized attention and adapt lessons to better meet the diverse needs of their students.

- **Tier 1 (Universal Support):** Small groups in Tier 1 allow for differentiation and help students who may need additional practice with core content. For instance, students who grasp the material quickly may benefit from small group enrichment activities, while others may need additional support to master foundational skills. Flexible grouping in Tier 1 helps ensure that all students are engaged and challenged appropriately.

- **Tier 2 (Targeted Support):** In Tier 2, small group instruction becomes more focused and targeted to address specific learning gaps. Teachers can use data from formative assessments or classroom observations to identify which students need additional support in specific areas. Small group work allows for more individualized attention and ensures that interventions are relevant to each student's needs.

- **Tier 3 (Intensive Support):** Small group instruction in Tier 3 is designed to provide intensive, individualized support for students who have not made adequate progress in the previous tiers. These groups are often smaller, and the instruction is highly tailored to address the specific needs of each student. Teachers can work on more specific interventions and use data to track progress, ensuring that students receive the support they need to catch up.

Using Data to Guide Tiered Instruction

An essential aspect of MTSS and tiered instruction is the use of data to guide decisions. Teachers should regularly collect and analyze data to determine which students need additional support and what kind of instruction will be most effective for them.

- **Progress Monitoring:** In Tier 2 and Tier 3, it is important to monitor students' progress regularly. Teachers should use data from quizzes, assignments, or formative assessments to track how well students are responding to interventions.

Small group instruction provides a great opportunity for this monitoring, as it allows teachers to assess students' understanding in real-time and adjust instruction as needed.
- **Adjusting Instruction:** Data helps teachers adjust instruction at each tier. If a student is not responding to Tier 2 interventions, the teacher can escalate the level of support and move them to Tier 3. Likewise, if a student is excelling in a Tier 1 group, the teacher can provide enrichment activities to further challenge them. Small group instruction enables teachers to make these adjustments quickly and effectively, ensuring that students receive the right level of support at the right time.

Best Practices for Integrating MTSS with Small Group Instruction

To maximize the effectiveness of small group instruction within the MTSS framework, consider the following best practices:

- **Collaborate with support staff:** If your school has intervention specialists or support staff, collaborate with them to ensure that interventions are appropriately aligned with MTSS. Support staff can help provide targeted strategies for Tier 2 and Tier 3 students and offer additional resources for small group instruction.
- **Use data to inform grouping decisions:** Whether you are using formative assessments, standardized test scores, or classroom observations, use data to determine how to group students effectively. Students who need similar types of support can be grouped together, while those who are excelling can work in groups with more advanced content or projects.
- **Regularly review progress:** Small group instruction should be flexible. Regularly review the progress of your small

groups, and adjust as needed. Some students may need to move to different groups as they progress, while others may require more time in the same group for additional support.

By integrating MTSS and tiered instruction with small group teaching, educators can ensure that every student receives the appropriate level of support to meet their unique learning needs. Small group instruction is a powerful way to personalize learning, close achievement gaps, and provide the targeted interventions students need to succeed academically.

You try it!: Incorporate **small group instruction** regularly in your classroom. Group students based on their needs, such as for enrichment or remediation. Use these small groups to provide tailored support, whether for struggling learners or for students who need additional challenges. Ensure that the rest of the class is engaged in independent or collaborative tasks during small group time to maximize learning.

Chapter 14: Building Stronger Connections – Effective Communication with Students and Parents

In secondary education, the connection between teachers, students, and parents often becomes more distant. As students progress through school, the focus shifts from foundational learning to more independent academic work, which can lead to a reduction in regular communication between home and school. In elementary education, teachers often send home newsletters, make regular phone calls, and communicate frequently with parents about student progress, successes, and challenges. Unfortunately, this level of communication often drops off as students enter secondary school.

However, the benefits of proactive, consistent communication, whether through newsletters, emails, phone calls, or face-to-face meetings, are immense. When teachers maintain a strong communication system with both students and parents, it fosters a greater sense of community, enhances student success, and creates an environment of support and encouragement for everyone involved. In this chapter, we will explore the importance of communication with both students and parents, how to implement strategies that build stronger connections, and the long-term impact of fostering these relationships.

The Importance of Communication in Secondary Education

Communication is not just about relaying information, it is about building relationships. When teachers communicate effectively with students and parents, they create a partnership that supports the overall development of the student. Regular communication helps build trust, keeps families informed about academic progress, and creates a space for addressing concerns before they become problems.

In secondary schools, students are often more independent, and teachers may assume that communication can be limited to report cards or emails only when there is an issue. However, regular, proactive communication has numerous benefits that directly impact student learning and emotional well-being:

- **Building Trust and Engagement:** Consistent communication shows students and parents that teachers are invested in their success. It helps build trust and fosters a partnership between home and school. When parents feel informed and involved, they are more likely to support their child's learning.
- **Enhancing Student Motivation:** Regular communication provides positive reinforcement for students. A simple check-in or a note home celebrating a student's success can increase motivation and boost self-esteem. When students see that their efforts are acknowledged, they feel more empowered to continue working hard.
- **Preventing Issues from Escalating:** By keeping the lines of communication open, teachers can address potential issues early, whether academic, behavioral, or social. This proactive approach prevents small problems from escalating and provides an opportunity for solutions before they become larger concerns.

Proactive vs. Reactive Communication

The difference between proactive and reactive communication is crucial. Reactive communication is typically limited to addressing problems or providing updates only when something goes wrong, such as sending home a report card or contacting parents about a disciplinary issue. While reactive communication is necessary, it is not enough to build a strong relationship or create a supportive learning environment.

Proactive communication, on the other hand, involves regularly reaching out to students and parents to provide updates, celebrate successes, and address potential challenges before they become problems. This type of communication creates an ongoing dialogue where both the teacher and the family feel involved in the educational process. It allows teachers to share not just problems but also positive progress and opportunities for growth.

Examples of proactive communication include:

- Regular newsletters or updates that highlight upcoming assignments, projects, and events.
- Positive phone calls or emails home, celebrating student achievements.
- Invitations for parents to participate in school activities, volunteering, or attending school events.
- Regular check-ins with students to gauge how they're doing academically and emotionally, offering support as needed.

Strategies for Communicating with Parents

In secondary education, it's essential to make communication with parents both efficient and meaningful. Here are several strategies for creating consistent and effective communication with parents:

- **Weekly or Biweekly Newsletters:** Send regular newsletters or emails to parents that provide updates on what's happening in class. Include information about upcoming assignments, tests, and events, as well as highlights of classroom successes. A simple, consistent format can make this task manageable and effective. This helps parents stay informed and feel engaged in their child's education.
- **Use of Digital Tools:** Many schools offer communication platforms like Google Classroom, Remind, or ClassDojo, which can be great tools for keeping parents up-to-date on

their child's progress. These tools allow teachers to send quick reminders, grades, or messages directly to parents in real time. When used regularly, they can help ensure parents feel connected to what's happening in the classroom.
- **Phone Calls and Personal Communication:** For more personal communication, a phone call to parents can make a significant impact. These calls don't always have to be about problems, regular calls to highlight a student's progress, acknowledge their hard work, or share successes are an excellent way to build strong, positive relationships with families.
- **Parent-Teacher Conferences:** While conferences are typically held a few times a year, they are an essential opportunity to communicate more in-depth about a student's progress. Make sure these meetings are collaborative and focused on solutions and growth, not just on issues. Consider offering virtual or flexible scheduling options to make it easier for parents to attend.

Fostering Student Communication Skills

In addition to fostering communication between teachers and parents, it's essential to help students develop strong communication skills. Encouraging students to take an active role in discussing their learning, asking for help when needed, and providing feedback to teachers helps them become more self-aware and independent learners.

- **Check-ins with Students:** Regular one-on-one check-ins with students provide an opportunity for teachers to discuss progress, challenges, and goals. These meetings can be informal, but they offer valuable insight into how students are feeling and where they may need additional support.

- **Encouraging Self-Advocacy:** Teach students how to advocate for themselves when they have concerns, need help, or want to share feedback. This helps build their confidence and responsibility for their own learning. Encourage them to reach out to you when they need clarification or assistance, and show them how to use communication tools like emails or office hours to discuss academic concerns.
- **Classroom Reflections:** Encourage students to reflect on their learning and share their thoughts regularly. Whether through journaling, surveys, or open discussions, giving students a platform to express their feelings about the classroom environment, assignments, or even social dynamics helps them develop communication and problem-solving skills.

Creating a Positive School Community

Communication between teachers, students, and parents plays a key role in creating a positive and supportive school community. When all parties are well-informed and engaged, the learning environment becomes a place of trust, collaboration, and shared goals.

- **Promote a Growth Mindset:** When communicating with both students and parents, emphasize a growth mindset. Celebrate progress, not just results, and encourage students to see challenges as opportunities for growth. This positive reinforcement creates an atmosphere where students feel empowered and motivated to reach their full potential.
- **Involve Parents in the Learning Process:** Encourage parents to be active participants in their child's education, whether by attending school events, helping with homework, or volunteering in the classroom. The more involved parents are, the stronger the partnership between home and school, which benefits the student's overall success.

- **Encourage Open Dialogue:** Encourage both students and parents to communicate openly with you about any issues, concerns, or needs that arise. Foster a classroom culture where feedback is welcomed and where everyone feels comfortable reaching out when support is needed.

Addressing Challenges in Communication

While communication is essential, there may be challenges that prevent effective dialogue. Barriers such as language differences, limited access to technology, or busy schedules can create obstacles to consistent communication. To overcome these challenges:

- **Offer Multiple Communication Channels:** Recognize that some families may prefer different communication methods. Offer multiple ways for parents to stay informed, whether through emails, phone calls, text messages, or school meetings.
- **Translate Materials:** If there are language barriers, provide translated materials or work with bilingual staff to ensure all parents can understand important information and feel included in the conversation.
- **Be Flexible with Meeting Times:** Understand that not all parents can attend meetings during traditional school hours. Offering flexible scheduling for conferences or using virtual platforms can help accommodate parents' busy schedules.

Effective communication is the cornerstone of building strong relationships between teachers, students, and parents. By making communication proactive, consistent, and inclusive, you can create a learning environment that fosters trust, engagement, and success for all students. Whether it's through newsletters, phone calls, or student check-ins, regular communication can strengthen the partnership between home and school, creating a supportive foundation for student

You try it!: Develop strong communication systems with both students and parents. Use tools like **ClassDojo** or **Google Classroom** to send regular updates. Send a weekly newsletter with upcoming assignments and important dates. Schedule periodic check-ins with students to offer encouragement and discuss any concerns. Additionally, set up parent-teacher conferences or meetings to involve families in their child's learning process and ensure they are informed and engaged.

Chapter 15: Modeling and Thinking Aloud – Making the Invisible Thinking Process Visible

In many secondary classrooms, teaching often focuses on the "what" of learning, the facts, the information, the answers. However, one crucial aspect of teaching that tends to be underutilized is the "how" of learning, the process by which students arrive at answers, analyze problems, and think critically. **Modeling** and **thinking aloud** are two powerful strategies that can bridge this gap, making the invisible thinking process visible and giving students a roadmap for how to approach tasks, solve problems, and engage with content more effectively.

Despite their importance, these strategies are often less common in secondary classrooms compared to elementary settings, where teachers frequently model behaviors and thinking aloud during lessons. But at the secondary level, students still benefit greatly from seeing how experts (i.e., their teachers) approach problems and tasks. Modeling helps to demystify complex content, teaches students to approach problems systematically, and reinforces the process of learning, not just the outcome.

The Importance of Modeling and Thinking Aloud

At its core, modeling and thinking aloud involve teachers demonstrating their thought processes out loud as they engage with the content. This could be in the form of solving a math problem, reading a text, writing an essay, or analyzing a historical event. The idea is simple: teachers make their thinking visible to students, providing a blueprint for how to approach similar tasks.

Research shows that **metacognitive strategies**, or thinking about one's thinking, are essential for student success. By hearing their teachers verbalize their thought processes, students learn how to approach problems, how to break tasks into manageable steps, and how to engage with content critically and thoughtfully. This is especially crucial in secondary education, where students are expected to engage with more complex materials and ideas.

Why Modeling and Thinking Aloud Are Rare in Secondary Classrooms

Many secondary teachers face the challenge of large class sizes, time constraints, and a focus on preparing students for standardized tests. As a result, there is often less emphasis on verbalizing the thinking process, which can seem time-consuming or redundant. Teachers may feel that students should be able to independently engage with content and solve problems on their own. However, research and classroom practices show that **modeling** the process of learning is essential for building critical thinking skills and boosting student success.

Another reason modeling and thinking aloud are infrequently used is the focus on outcomes rather than processes. Teachers may place greater emphasis on teaching students the right answers or the correct methods, instead of demonstrating how those answers or methods are arrived at. This shift in focus can limit students' opportunities to develop deeper understanding and critical problem-solving skills.

The Benefits of Modeling and Thinking Aloud

Modeling and thinking aloud offer several benefits that enhance learning outcomes, particularly in secondary education:

1. **Clarifies Complex Concepts**
   When a teacher models how to break down and solve a problem, they help students see how abstract or complex concepts can be made more accessible. For example, when analyzing a difficult passage from Shakespeare or solving a calculus problem, seeing the teacher's step-by-step process can clarify the method and make it more manageable.
2. **Fosters Metacognition**
   Modeling helps students think about their own thinking. By observing how a teacher approaches a task, students gain insight into the decision-making process. This encourages students to reflect on their own strategies and improve their problem-solving skills.
3. **Builds Problem-Solving Skills**
   When teachers model problem-solving aloud, they demonstrate the cognitive steps needed to approach a challenge. Students learn to break down a problem, analyze it from different angles, and apply appropriate strategies, all critical skills that they can use in their own work.
4. **Increases Student Confidence**
   Students often struggle with tasks because they are uncertain about how to approach them. By seeing the teacher model the process, students gain confidence that they too can engage with and succeed at similar tasks. Modeling provides reassurance and shows that it's okay to make mistakes during the learning process.
5. **Enhances Engagement**
   When teachers model their thought processes and actively engage with the content aloud, students are more likely to stay focused. This dynamic interaction creates a learning environment where students are active participants, not passive listeners. It draws them into the material in a way that traditional lectures may not.

How to Model Effectively

To effectively incorporate modeling and thinking aloud into your teaching, consider the following strategies:

1. **Think-Aloud in Problem-Solving**
   Use the "think-aloud" strategy when solving problems, whether they are math equations, analyzing literature, or evaluating a scientific theory. As you solve a problem, verbalize each step you take, the questions you ask yourself, and the reasoning behind your decisions. For example, when solving a math word problem, you might say, "First, I notice that the problem is asking for the area, which means I need to use the area formula. Now, I'll identify the given values and plug them into the equation..."

2. **Modeling Writing and Reading**
   While reading or writing, model how you engage with the material. For example, during a reading assignment, you can read a passage aloud and stop to think aloud about the meaning, structure, and any difficult vocabulary. When writing an essay, show students how to brainstorm, organize ideas, and draft a thesis statement. Talk about your thinking at each stage of the process.

3. **Show How You Tackle Challenges**
   As you model, don't shy away from showing how you tackle difficulties. For example, when analyzing a complex text, acknowledge parts of it that confuse you, and talk through how you figure them out. This reinforces the idea that learning is a process that involves trial, error, and reflection.

4. **Modeling Classroom Expectations**
   Teachers can also use modeling to demonstrate expected classroom behaviors. Whether it's how to ask for help, participate in group work, or provide constructive feedback

to peers, think aloud about how you want students to engage with each other and the material.

Practical Application Ideas

1. **Start with Short Think-Alouds**
   Introduce short bursts of thinking aloud throughout your lessons. For example, when solving a math problem on the board or analyzing a text with your class, stop at key points to explain your thinking. Gradually build up these moments until they become a regular part of your teaching.
2. **Create Opportunities for Students to Model**
   Once you've modeled a process, give students opportunities to try it themselves, either independently or in groups. Ask students to "think aloud" as they work through a problem or analyze a piece of text, which reinforces the modeling process and helps them internalize the strategies.
3. **Modeling During Group Work**
   As students work in groups, circulate the room and provide "mini think-aloud" demonstrations. For example, when a group is struggling with a question, walk them through the process aloud, asking questions and demonstrating how to approach the task.
4. **Use Video or Recorded Demonstrations**
   For more complex tasks, consider recording yourself modeling the process and showing it to students as a reference. This can be especially helpful for students who may need more time or for reviewing key steps in a process.

Common Mistakes to Avoid

- **Don't Over-Explain**: While think-alouds are important, over-explaining can lead to confusion. Keep your explanations clear and concise, focusing on key steps and reasoning.
- **Avoid Making It Too Formulaic**: While consistency is important, don't make your modeling sessions feel robotic. Let your personality and authentic problem-solving process shine through to keep students engaged.

Modeling and thinking aloud are essential tools for making the learning process visible and accessible. By demonstrating how you think through problems, analyze content, and approach tasks, you help students build the critical thinking skills they need to succeed. These strategies may take time to implement, but the results, engaged, confident, and capable students, are well worth the effort. Start small, be consistent, and watch your students grow in their ability to think critically and independently.

You try it!; Incorporate **modeling and think-alouds** in your lessons, especially for complex tasks like reading comprehension, problem-solving, and writing. As you demonstrate your thinking process, explain each step in detail to show students how experts approach the task. Encourage students to practice think-alouds themselves, allowing them to make their thinking visible and clarify their reasoning.

Chapter 16: Implementing Change – Overcoming Resistance to Adapting Elementary Strategies in Secondary Education

Adapting elementary strategies for secondary classrooms can feel like a significant shift, especially when educators are accustomed to traditional methods of teaching. Teachers may resist change for a variety of reasons, including comfort with existing routines, concerns about time constraints, and uncertainty about how younger teaching methods will work with older students. However, the evidence is clear: strategies commonly used in elementary classrooms, such as manipulatives, group seating, interactive activities, and visual aids, can benefit secondary students just as much as they benefit younger learners.

In this chapter, we will explore how to successfully implement these changes in secondary classrooms, address common sources of resistance, and encourage both teachers and students to embrace a more dynamic, engaging approach to learning. The focus will be on practical strategies for easing this transition, fostering buy-in from educators, and demonstrating the value of these strategies in promoting student success.

Understanding the Roots of Resistance

Resistance to change is natural, especially in environments where traditions and established practices have been in place for a long time. In secondary education, many teachers have honed their craft using lecture-based instruction, assessments, and assignments that focus on individual learning. When asked to embrace strategies that might be perceived as "elementary," some teachers may feel that these approaches are not appropriate for older students or are incompatible with the demands of high school-level curricula. Here are some common reasons why teachers may resist adapting these strategies:

- **Comfort with established routines:** Teachers who have been successful using traditional methods often feel that these methods are working, and therefore may be hesitant to shift to new strategies that feel unfamiliar or untested.
- **Time constraints:** Secondary teachers are often pressed for time due to packed curriculums, exam schedules, and the need to prepare students for standardized tests. Teachers may worry that adopting more hands-on or interactive strategies will take away from valuable instructional time.
- **Perceived mismatch with student maturity:** Teachers may believe that secondary students are beyond the need for manipulatives, group activities, or visual aids. They may assume that older students prefer lectures and individual tasks rather than the more engaging, interactive methods often seen in elementary classrooms.

Recognizing these barriers is essential in addressing them and guiding the transition toward more dynamic teaching practices. When teachers understand the value of these strategies and how they can be adapted for secondary education, they are more likely to embrace them.

Building Buy-In Among Educators

The first step in overcoming resistance is to help educators understand the benefits of using elementary strategies in secondary classrooms. Teachers need to feel supported, equipped, and confident that these strategies will enhance student learning. Here are some strategies for building support for this change:

- **Provide evidence and success stories:** Teachers are more likely to embrace change if they can see that it works. Share research, case studies, and success stories from other secondary teachers who have successfully used elementary strategies. Highlight the positive impact these strategies have had on student engagement, achievement, and classroom culture. Seeing concrete examples of success can make the benefits feel more tangible.

- **Offer professional development and resources:** Professional development is a key element in helping teachers feel prepared to incorporate new strategies into their classrooms. Provide training sessions that demonstrate how these elementary strategies can be adapted to the secondary level. Ensure that these sessions are hands-on, offering practical tools and techniques that teachers can immediately implement in their own classrooms. Additionally, offer resources, such as lesson plans, templates, and materials, so teachers feel supported as they transition.
- **Start small and allow for gradual change:** Rather than expecting teachers to completely overhaul their teaching methods overnight, start by encouraging small changes. For example, teachers can begin by incorporating group seating or interactive activities into one or two lessons a week. Once teachers see how these strategies improve student engagement, they will be more likely to embrace them on a larger scale.
- **Foster collaboration and peer support:** Encourage collaboration among teachers who are using these strategies successfully and those who are hesitant to try them. Teachers can observe each other's classrooms, share best practices, and provide support as they experiment with new methods. Peer collaboration is a powerful way to build confidence and demonstrate the effectiveness of these strategies.

Addressing Time Constraints and Curriculum Demands

One of the biggest concerns that secondary teachers have about adapting these strategies is that they will take away from instructional time needed to meet curriculum requirements or prepare students for standardized assessments. However, it is possible to integrate engaging, interactive strategies into the curriculum without sacrificing essential content. Here's how:

- **Integrating strategies into existing lessons:** Instead of viewing these strategies as separate activities or add-ons, encourage teachers to weave them into their regular lessons. For example, instead of using lecture-style instruction for an entire period, teachers can break up the lesson with group discussions, activities, or hands-on tasks that reinforce key concepts. By blending these strategies into the curriculum, teachers can maintain the focus on essential content while enhancing student engagement and understanding.
- **Making learning more efficient and impactful:** While interactive strategies may take slightly more time upfront, they can make the learning process more efficient in the long run. For example, using small group instruction or manipulatives to explain complex concepts can help students grasp the material faster, leading to less time spent re-teaching or reviewing later. The goal is to increase student mastery of the content, which ultimately leads to more efficient use of instructional time.
- **Emphasizing quality over quantity:** Encourage teachers to focus on the quality of student engagement and understanding, rather than rushing through the material to cover every single topic. By incorporating more engaging and interactive strategies, students are more likely to retain and apply what they've learned, which leads to better overall outcomes. Quality instruction, even if it covers fewer topics,

often produces better results than simply covering more material in a superficial way.

Adapting Strategies for Older Students

While elementary strategies may initially seem too "young" for older students, the truth is that secondary students still benefit from these engaging methods. The key is to adapt these strategies to suit the maturity and developmental stage of the students. Here are some ways to make elementary strategies work for secondary learners:

- **Incorporate higher-level thinking tasks:** Instead of using simple manipulatives or group activities, adapt them to encourage higher-level thinking. For example, use manipulatives in mathematics or science to explore complex theories or models, or ask students to work in groups to analyze and solve real-world problems. This will ensure that the activities are challenging and engaging for older students.
- **Use technology to enhance strategies:** Many elementary strategies, such as interactive notebooks or group activities, can be enhanced by technology. Encourage teachers to incorporate digital tools like Google Classroom, Padlet, or Kahoot to make activities more engaging and interactive. These tools are widely used in secondary classrooms and can help make elementary strategies feel more relevant to older students.
- **Relate activities to real-world applications:** Secondary students are more likely to engage with strategies that have real-world relevance. Show them how manipulatives, group work, or hands-on activities are used in real-life situations, such as in professional fields, research, or the workforce. By making these activities relevant to their lives, students will see the value of interactive learning.

The Long-Term Benefits of Embracing Change

The shift toward more interactive, engaging teaching methods may feel challenging at first, but the long-term benefits are immense. These strategies can lead to more motivated, engaged students who are better prepared for college, careers, and life beyond school. By adopting elementary strategies, teachers can create a classroom environment that fosters creativity, collaboration, critical thinking, and problem-solving, skills that are essential for success in today's world.

The key to success is building a culture of openness, collaboration, and continuous improvement. When teachers are supported in their transition and given the tools and resources they need, they can confidently implement new strategies that will ultimately benefit both their students and themselves. The classroom of tomorrow is one where learning is personalized, engaging, and relevant, a place where students feel motivated and empowered to reach their full potential.

You try it!: When implementing new strategies, like **group seating** or active learning techniques, start small. Make gradual adjustments and gather feedback from your students. Share success stories with colleagues to encourage buy-in, and be prepared to address concerns with evidence of how these changes benefit student engagement and achievement. Remember, change takes time, and small wins will pave the way for larger shifts in teaching practices.

Conclusion: Bringing It All Together – The Power of Reconnecting Elementary Strategies to Secondary Education

As we conclude this journey through the strategies and frameworks that can elevate secondary education, it's important to reflect on the core message of this book: the value of reconnecting the engagement techniques and learning strategies used in elementary education to the secondary classroom.

Throughout this book, we have explored various methods, ranging from manipulatives and anchor charts to small group instruction and interactive learning tools, that have long been proven to support the development of young minds. What often gets lost as students move into secondary education is the idea that these strategies lose their relevance. However, as we have seen, these strategies are not just for younger students; they have the power to engage, challenge, and inspire secondary learners in profound ways.

By introducing strategies like collaborative seating, active learning, frequent checks for understanding, and the integration of MTSS, we can create a learning environment where students are not only prepared for standardized tests, but are also equipped with the skills they need for success beyond the classroom. These skills, critical thinking, collaboration, creativity, and communication, are essential for students to thrive in an increasingly interconnected and complex world.

The Benefits of Change: Why Adapting Strategies Is Worth It

The transition to a more dynamic, student-centered approach to secondary education may seem daunting, especially when working within the constraints of time, curriculum, and perceived student maturity. Yet, the benefits of embracing these strategies are undeniable. When we take the time to introduce methods that engage students actively, we are doing more than just fostering academic achievement, we are cultivating a classroom culture of curiosity, confidence, and ownership of learning.

By reconnecting with strategies from elementary education, we are also reminding ourselves as educators that learning is not just a one-way transfer of information from teacher to student. Learning is a shared process, a dynamic experience where students take part in their own education, where they collaborate with their peers, and where they engage with content in ways that make it meaningful to them.

Building a Classroom Culture of Engagement, Collaboration, and Growth

The transformation towards a more engaging classroom doesn't happen overnight, and it requires effort, patience, and commitment from educators, students, and the entire school community. The tools and strategies discussed in this book, whether they be small group instruction, vocabulary walls, or differentiated assessments, are not just tactics to improve lesson delivery; they are part of creating a classroom culture of mutual respect, growth, and engagement.

When students feel connected to the material and know their voices matter, they are more likely to take an active role in their education. This shift in mindset can lead to improved academic outcomes, higher levels of student motivation, and a greater sense of belonging within the classroom.

As we've explored in chapters like **Using Data to Inform Instruction**, **Checking for Understanding**, and **Small Group Instruction**, effective teaching requires constant adaptation. It requires tuning into the needs of our students, being flexible with our methods, and continuously seeking ways to improve our craft. This is not just about what we teach, but how we teach, how we listen, and how we engage.

The Future of Education: A Student-Centered Approach

Looking ahead, it's clear that the future of education lies in creating environments that are both nurturing and challenging, where students are active participants in their learning, where diverse needs are met with targeted support, and where every student is given the opportunity to succeed.

The strategies we've discussed here are just the beginning. The possibilities are endless as we continue to explore new ways to integrate technology, foster creativity, and build inclusive classrooms. However, the foundation remains the same: student engagement, personalized learning, and the belief that every student is capable of growth when given the right tools, support, and encouragement.

As educators, we must remember that the tools we use are not just methods, they are investments in the futures of our students. By adopting these strategies, we are laying the groundwork for a generation of learners who are prepared not only for the challenges of today's world, but for the ones they will face tomorrow.

Final Thoughts

Reconnecting elementary strategies with secondary education is not about simplifying the curriculum or "dumbing down" the content, it's about fostering a richer, more engaging learning experience for students. It's about recognizing that students at every level, whether they are in kindergarten or high school, need to feel connected to their learning, be challenged in meaningful ways, and have opportunities to reflect, collaborate, and grow.

As you move forward in your teaching journey, remember that the tools and strategies discussed here are meant to empower you as an educator. By embracing these methods, you are not just improving your classroom instruction, you are changing the lives of your students, equipping them with the skills, knowledge, and confidence to succeed in the world beyond school.

The future of education is in your hands, and by embracing these strategies, you are playing a pivotal role in shaping that future.

Appendix: Shopping List for Teachers

General Classroom Resources

- **Classroom supplies**:
    - Whiteboard markers (for visual aids, modeling)
    - Sticky notes (for interactive activities and checking for understanding)
    - Highlighter pens (for emphasizing key concepts during reading or note-taking)
    - Post-it pads (for quick formative assessments or brainstorming)
    - Chart paper (for creating anchor charts and visual organizers)
    - Markers, pens, and index cards (for vocabulary walls, student feedback)

Chapter 1: The Power of Engagement – Connecting with Every Student

- **Interactive tools**:
    - Clickers or polling software (e.g., Kahoot!, Poll Everywhere) for quick formative assessments
    - Digital collaboration platforms (e.g., Google Classroom, Padlet)
    - Project-based learning kits (for hands-on group projects)
- **Classroom setup**:
    - Flexible seating options (e.g., bean bags, adjustable desks, standing desks)

Chapter 2: Visual Learning – Why Secondary Classrooms Should Be Vibrant

- **Visual aids**:
    - Laminated visuals (charts, diagrams, concept maps)
    - Projector or interactive whiteboard (for displaying visuals and multimedia)
    - Visual organizers (mind maps, Venn diagrams, graphic organizers)
- **Technology**:
    - Multimedia software (e.g., Prezi, Google Slides, Canva for creating and presenting visuals)
    - Document cameras (for displaying student work or visual aids)

Chapter 3: Personalization – Making Learning Relevant for Every Student

- **Differentiation tools**:
    - Learning preference surveys (e.g., VARK Questionnaire to identify student learning styles)
    - Adaptive learning software (e.g., DreamBox, Khan Academy, IXL for personalized practice)
    - Personalized learning platforms (e.g., Google Classroom for self-paced assignments)
- **Classroom resources**:
    - Learning contracts or choice boards for student autonomy
    - Personalized assignment templates to allow choice in projects

Chapter 4: From Lecture to Interaction – Creating Active Learning Spaces

- **Active learning tools**:
    - Collaborative seating arrangements (e.g., desks in clusters or U-shapes for group work)
    - Digital collaboration platforms (e.g., Padlet, Google Docs for group brainstorming)
    - Interactive whiteboards for dynamic lessons and student participation
- **Student feedback**:
    - Exit ticket templates (paper or digital) to gauge student understanding

Chapter 5: Manipulatives, Anchor Charts, and Other Tools for Understanding at Any Age

- **Manipulatives**:
    - Math manipulatives (e.g., base-10 blocks, fraction tiles, geoboards)
    - Science kits (for hands-on exploration of concepts)
    - Literacy manipulatives (e.g., letter tiles, sentence strips)
- **Anchor chart materials**:
    - Large poster boards and adhesive paper for creating and displaying anchor charts
    - Visual templates for creating graphic organizers
    - Colored pens for group contributions to anchor charts

Chapter 6: Vocabulary Walls and Word Walls – Building Language at Every Level

- **Vocabulary wall materials**:
    - Large poster boards or bulletin board space for creating word walls
    - Magnetic letters or word cards for interactive vocabulary wall activities
    - Index cards for creating student flashcards for vocabulary practice
- **Vocabulary development tools**:
    - Digital tools for vocabulary building (e.g., Quizlet for flashcards and quizzes)
    - Dictionaries (physical or digital) for students to reference
    - Vocabulary enrichment books (e.g., *Word Power Made Easy* by Norman Lewis)

Chapter 7: The Power of Grouped Seating – Collaborative Learning in Secondary Classrooms

- **Seating arrangements**:
    - Collaborative seating furniture (e.g., tables instead of desks, group seating)
    - Flexible seating options (e.g., floor cushions, stools, low tables)
- **Collaboration tools**:
    - Whiteboard tables (for group brainstorming or problem-solving)
    - Group project folders or digital collaboration tools (e.g., Google Docs for group writing)

Chapter 8: Read-Alouds – Engaging Minds Across All Ages

- **Read-aloud books**:
    - High-interest, age-appropriate books for read-aloud sessions (both fiction and nonfiction)
    - Audiobook subscriptions (e.g., Audible, OverDrive for listening along)
- **Reading tools**:
    - High-quality audio equipment for playing audiobooks (if necessary)
    - Timer (for pacing and managing read-aloud time effectively)

Chapter 9: Highlighters, Post-Its, and Interactive Notebooks – Creating Tools for Active Learning

- **Active learning tools**:
    - Interactive notebooks (physical or digital templates)
    - Sticky notes for annotation and reflection
    - Highlighter pens for student engagement and visual emphasis
- **Reflection tools**:
    - Journals for students to reflect on their learning after lessons
    - Templates for student-led note-taking or annotations

Chapter 10: Using Data to Inform Instruction

- **Assessment tools**:
    - Formative assessment software (e.g., Quizlet, Google Forms, Socrative for quizzes and polls)

- o Data tracking sheets or software (e.g., Google Sheets, Excel for tracking progress)
- o Digital formative assessment tools for quick checks for understanding (e.g., Kahoot!)
- **Student progress tracking**:
  - o Rubrics for assessing student learning and progress
  - o Visual charts for monitoring individual or class-wide performance

Chapter 11: Checking for Understanding – Strategies to Gauge Student Learning

- **Formative assessment tools**:
  - o Quick exit ticket systems (paper or digital tools like Google Forms or Exit Ticket apps)
  - o Clickers or polling systems (e.g., Kahoot!, Poll Everywhere for immediate feedback)
- **Feedback tools**:
  - o Peer review templates (printed or digital forms for peer feedback)
  - o Rubrics for consistent and clear feedback

Chapter 12: Small Group Instruction – Tailoring Learning to Meet Student Needs

- **Group activities materials**:
  - o Small group task cards (with prompts or questions for group work)
  - o Group project kits (materials for creating posters, models, or presentations)
- **Instructional support tools**:

- o Timer (to manage time and keep small group work focused)
- o Personalized learning software for small group use (e.g., IXL, DreamBox, Lexia)

Chapter 13: Building Stronger Connections – Effective Communication with Students and Parents

- **Communication tools**:
  - o Email templates for regular parent communication
  - o Newsletters (digital or printed) for weekly updates
  - o Parent-teacher conference scheduling software (e.g., SignUpGenius, Conference Scheduler)
- **Engagement platforms**:
  - o Classroom communication platforms (e.g., Remind, ClassDojo, Google Classroom)

Chapter 14: Modeling and Thinking Aloud – Making the Invisible Thinking Process Visible

- **Modeling tools**:
  - o Whiteboards or document cameras for demonstrating problem-solving steps
  - o Visual aids for modeling reading or writing processes (e.g., sentence frames, annotated texts)
- **Student engagement**:
  - o Question prompts for encouraging students to think aloud during group activities
  - o Graphic organizers for mapping out thinking processes

Chapter 15: Implementing Change – Overcoming Resistance to Adapting Elementary Strategies in Secondary Education

- **Change management resources**:
    - Professional development books on educational change (e.g., *Leading Change* by John Kotter)
    - Video conferencing tools (e.g., Zoom, Microsoft Teams) for collaborative professional learning
- **Teacher reflection tools**:
    - Reflective teaching journals or software (e.g., Google Docs, Evernote for documenting changes)
    - Surveys or feedback tools for evaluating changes (e.g., SurveyMonkey, Google Forms)

General Classroom Tech & Resources

- **Technology tools**:
    - Interactive whiteboards (e.g., SMART Boards or Promethean Boards)
    - Document cameras for displaying student work and think-aloud demonstrations
    - Tablets or laptops for individual or group research (e.g., iPads, Chromebooks)
    - Video recording equipment for capturing think-aloud or modeling sessions

Recommended Reading and Resources

These resources informed the strategies and perspectives shared in this book.

Beck, I. L., McKeown, M. G., Kucan, L. (2002). Bringing Words to Life: Robust Vocabulary Instruction. United Kingdom: Guilford Publications.

Black, P., & Wiliam, D. (1998). Inside the black box: Raising standards through classroom assessment. *Phi Delta Kappan, 80*(2), 139-148. https://doi.org/10.1177/003172171009200119

Flavell, J. H. (1979). Metacognition and cognitive monitoring: A new area of cognitive–developmental inquiry. *American Psychologist, 34*(10), 906-911. https://doi.org/10.1037/0003-066X.34.10.906

Fredricks, J., Blumenfeld, P., & Paris, A. (2004). School engagement: Potential of the concept, state of the evidence. *Review of Educational Research, 74*(1), 59-109. https://doi.org/10.3102/00346543074001059

Fullan, M. (2007). *The new meaning of educational change* (4th ed.). Teachers College Press.

Guthrie, J. T., & Wigfield, A. (2000). *Engagement and motivation in reading.* Lawrence Erlbaum Associates.

Hattie, J. (2012). Visible learning for teachers: Maximizing impact on learning. Routledge.

Johnson, D. W., & Johnson, R. T. (1999). Making cooperative learning work. *Theory Into Practice, 38*(2), 67-73. https://doi.org/10.1080/00405849909543834

Mayer, R. E. (2005). *The Cambridge handbook of multimedia learning.* Cambridge University Press.

Pashler, H., Rohrer, D., Cepeda, N. J., & Carpenter, S. K. (2007). Enhancing learning and study strategies. *Psychonomic Bulletin & Review, 14*(2), 227-233. https://doi.org/10.3758/BF03194065

Pressley, M., & Afflerbach, P. (1995). *Verbal protocols of reading: The nature of constructively responsive reading.* Lawrence Erlbaum Associates.

Rieber, L. P. (1996). The effects of visual and verbal annotation on students' problem-solving performance. *Educational Technology Research and Development, 44*(4), 5-17.
https://doi.org/10.1007/BF02300440

Rosenshine, B. (2012). Principles of instruction: Research-based strategies that all teachers should know. *American Educator, 36*(1), 12-20. https://www.aft.org/ae/spring2012/rosenshine

Slavin, R. E. (2015). Cooperative learning in elementary schools. Education 3-13, 43(1), 5-14. https://doi.org/10.1080/03004279.2015.963370.

Sweller, J. (1988). Cognitive load during problem solving: Effects on learning. *Cognitive Science, 12*(2), 257-285.
https://doi.org/10.1207/s15516709cog1202_4

Tomlinson, C. A. (2014). The differentiated classroom: Responding to the needs of all learners. Ascd.

Vygotsky, L. S. (1978). Mind in Society: Development of Higher Psychological Processes (M. Cole, V. Jolm-Steiner, S. Scribner, & E. Souberman, Eds.). Harvard University Press. https://doi.org/10.2307/j.ctvjf9vz4

Wood, D., Bruner, J. S., & Ross, G. (1976). The role of tutoring in problem solving. *Journal of Child Psychology and Psychiatry, 17*(2), 89-100. https://doi.org/10.1111/j.1469-7610.1976.tb00381.x

Acknowledgments

I want to thank the educators who have shaped my practice from the start. Your hard work and care for students influence every chapter of this book. I am grateful for the colleagues and leaders who supported my ideas, encouraged me to write, and reminded me of the purpose behind this work.

To the teachers I have coached and the teams I have led, thank you for trusting me and giving your best each day. To the students I have taught across grade levels and across the world, your energy and honesty continue to guide how I think about learning.

I thank my family, especially my daughter, Anyka Starr, for the support, patience, and love that made this project possible. You have always believed in every step I take, and I carry that with me.

About the Author

Dr. Pamela Chandler is an experienced educator and leader with a passion for transforming classrooms and fostering student success. With a background as an elementary educator, Dr. Chandler has a deep understanding of the importance of engagement, creativity, and active learning in the classroom. She has spent over two decades in education, working at various levels to support teachers and students.

Currently serving as the Principal of a K-12 school, Dr. Chandler brings a wealth of experience to her role. Her work spans a wide range of educational settings, where she has championed the integration of innovative teaching strategies and data-driven decision-making to enhance learning outcomes for all students.

As a passionate advocate for bridging the gap between elementary and secondary education, Dr. Chandler believes that the skills and strategies used in elementary classrooms should be adapted and implemented at all grade levels. Her leadership has helped cultivate inclusive, student-centered environments where every student can thrive, and she continues to inspire educators to create classrooms that are dynamic, engaging, and responsive to the needs of all learners.

www.ingramcontent.com/pod-product-compliance
Lightning Source LLC
LaVergne TN
LVHW020438070526
838199LV00063B/4776